ROYAL
LONDON GUIDE
& STREETFINDER

A Nicholson Guide

First published 1987

© Robert Nicholson Publications 1987

Text by Judy Allen
Design by Bob Vickers

Central London street maps
© Robert Nicholson Publications based
upon the Ordnance Survey with the
sanction of the Controller of Her Majesty's
Stationery Office. Crown Copyright
reserved.

Original design Robert Nicholson and
Romek Marber.

London Underground Map by kind
permission of London Transport.

All other maps
© Robert Nicholson Publications

Robert Nicholson Publications
16 Golden Square
London W1R 4BN

Great care has been taken throughout this
book to be accurate but the publishers
cannot accept responsibility for any errors
which appear, or their consequences.

Typeset by Rowland Phototypesetting Ltd,
Bury St Edmunds, Suffolk

Printed in Great Britain by
John Bartholomew and Son Ltd,
Edinburgh

ISBN 0 94 857610 3
87/1/110

Symbols

Symbol	Description
†	Church
✚	Hospital
🚗	Car park
🏛	Historic buildings
⌂	Small buildings
⚑	Schools
⬤	Sports stadium
⊖	London Underground station
⬛	British Rail station
▬	Coach station
✈	Air terminal
⇥	British Rail terminal
PO	Post office
Pol	Police station
→	One ways
⋯⋯	Footpath
☰	Thames Water Authority piers
50 ▶ ◀ 100	Figure indicating the direction of street numbering and the approximate position
	Park, Golf course, Sports field, Recreation ground, Garden
	Cemetery, Allotment, Heath, Down, Open space

Large scale   Central area

½ mile

½ km

ROBERT NICHOLSON PUBLICATIONS

CONTENTS

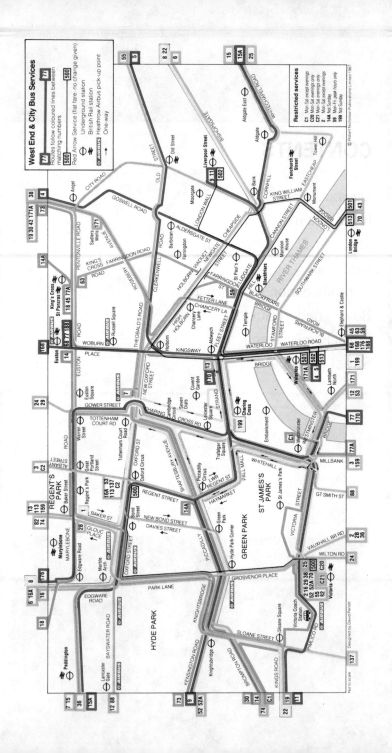

West End & City Bus Services

Routes follow coloured lines between matching numbers

500 Red Arrow Service (flat fare - no change given)

Underground station

British Rail station

Heathrow Airbus pick-up point

One-way

Restricted services

C1 Mon-Sat except evenings only
C20 Mon-Sat evenings only
C21 Mon-Sat evenings only
2 Mon-Sat except evenings
14A Not Sunday
59 Mon-Fri peak hours only
199 Not Sunday

© Robert Nicholson Publications Limited 1987

Not to scale

Designed by David Perrott

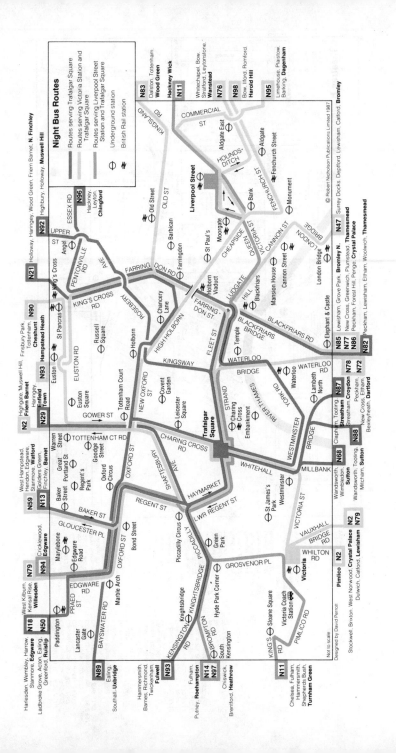

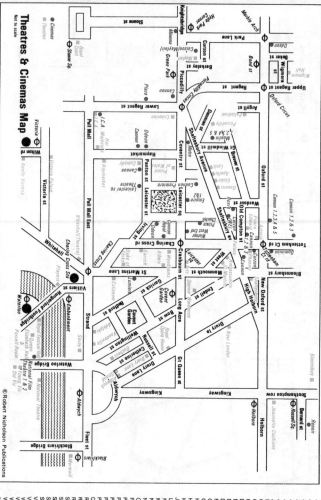

Theatres & Cinemas Map

Not to scale

● Cinemas
■ Theatres

© Robert Nicholson Publications

KEY MAP

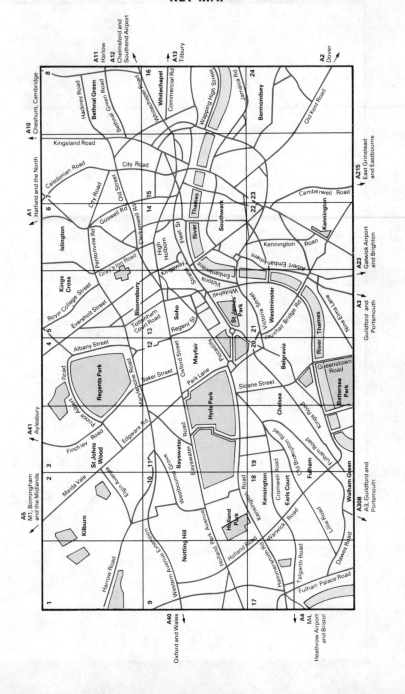

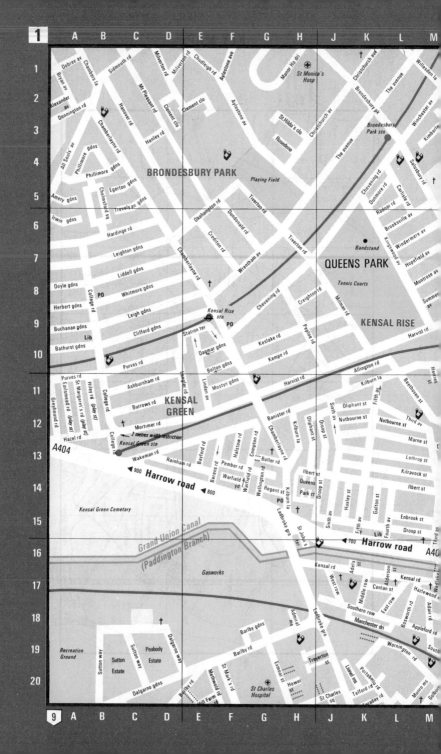

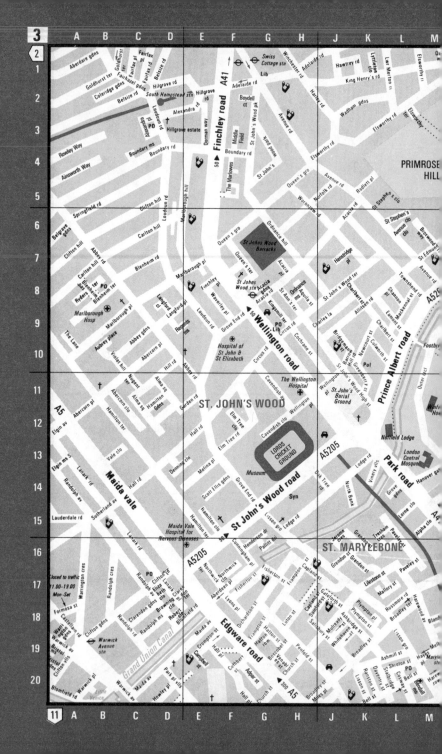

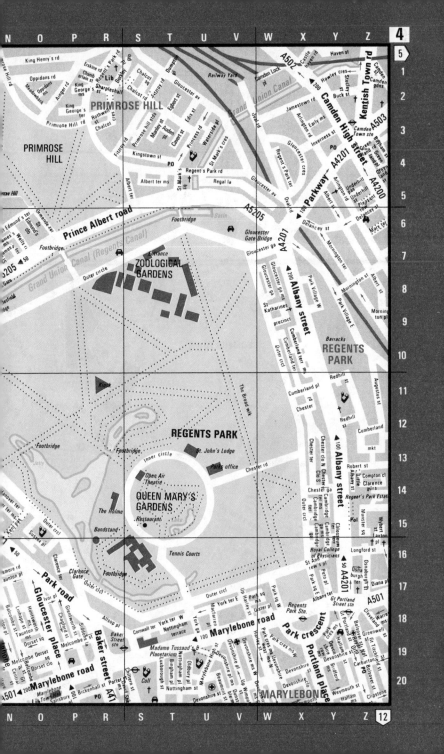

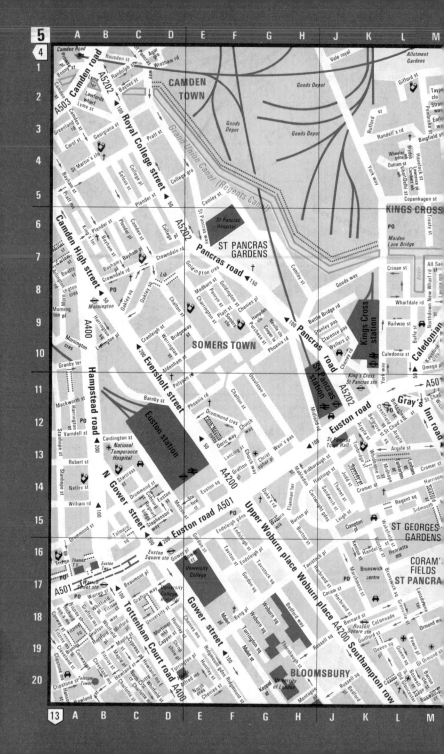

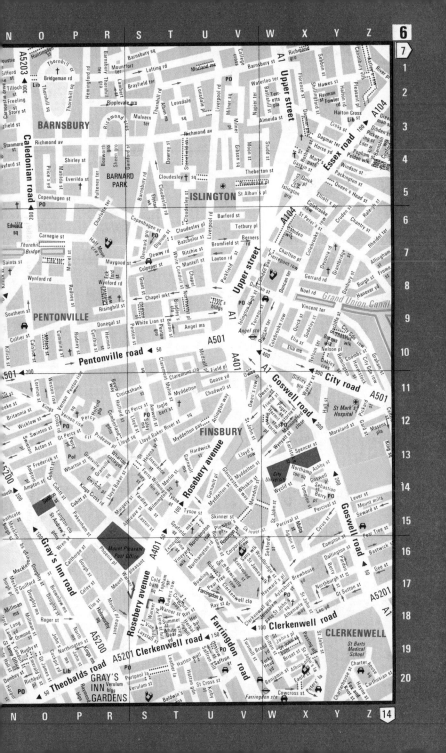

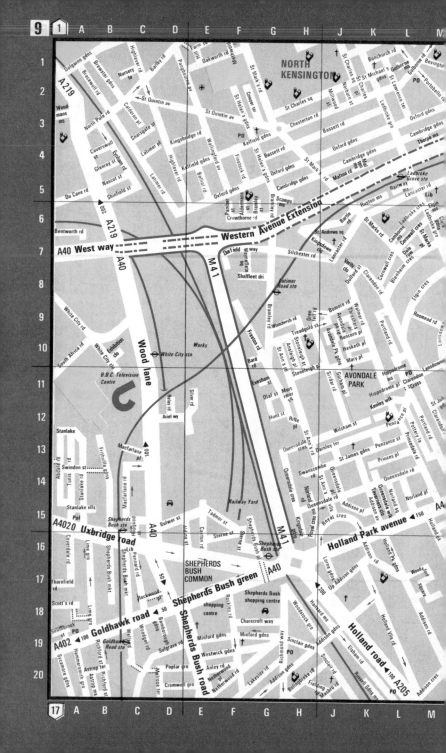

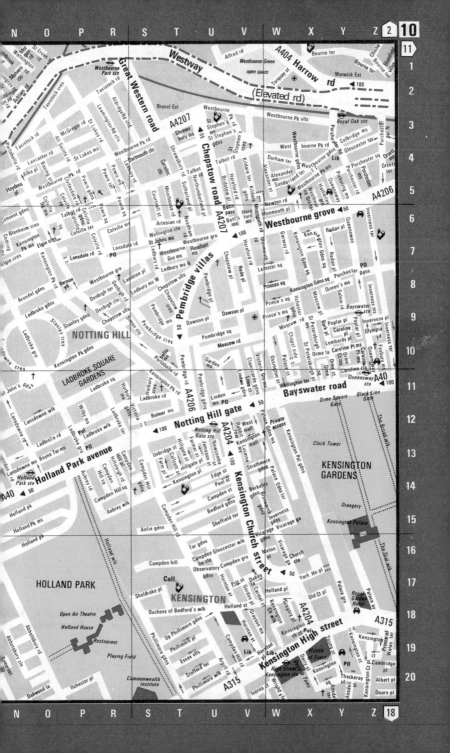

A B C D E F G H J K L M

10

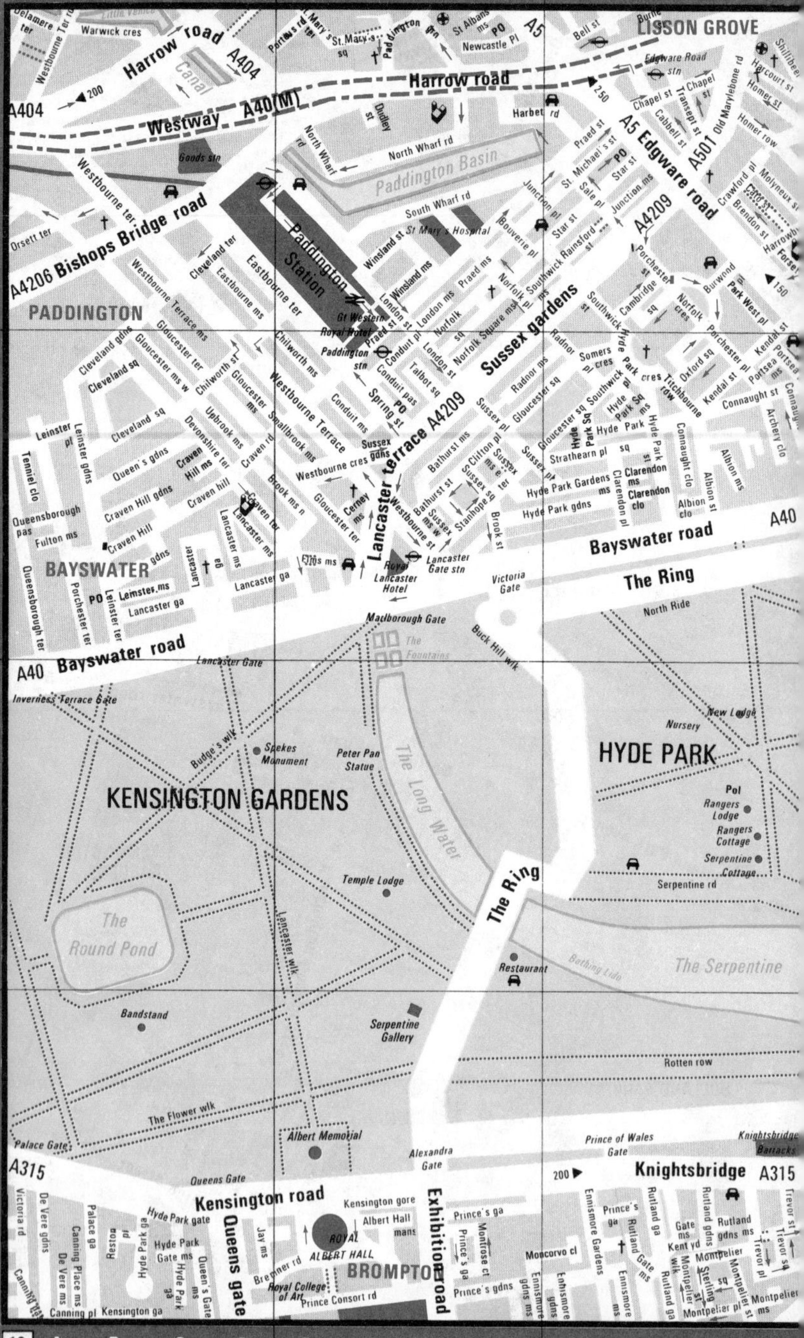

LISSON GROVE
PADDINGTON
BAYSWATER
KENSINGTON GARDENS
HYDE PARK
BROMPTON
Harrow road
Westway
A40(M)
A404
Canal
Goods stn
Paddington Basin
North Wharf rd
South Wharf rd
St Mary's Hospital
Paddington Station
Gt Western Royal Hotel
Paddington stn
A4206 Bishops Bridge road
Westbourne ter
Eastbourne ter
Cleveland ter
Westbourne Terrace
Sussex gardens
Lancaster terrace A4209
A5 Edgware road
A501 Old Marylebone rd
Edgware Road stn
Bell st
Praed st
Norfolk sq
Cleveland sq
Cleveland gdns
Gloucester ter
Leinster gdns
Queen's gdns
Craven hill
Craven Hill gdns
Craven Hill
Queensborough ter
Porchester ter
Lancaster ga
Lancaster Gate stn
Royal Lancaster Hotel
Hyde Park Gardens
Hyde Park gdns
Connaught st
A40
Bayswater road
The Ring
Victoria Gate
Marlborough Gate
The Fountains
Lancaster Gate
Inverness Terrace Gate
Buck Hill wlk
North Ride
New Lodge
Nursery
Budge's wlk
Spekes Monument
Peter Pan Statue
The Long Water
Pol
Rangers Lodge
Rangers Cottage
Serpentine Cottage
Serpentine rd
Temple Lodge
The Round Pond
Lancaster wlk
Restaurant
Bathing Lido
The Serpentine
Bandstand
Serpentine Gallery
Rotten row
The Flower wlk
Albert Memorial
Palace Gate
Prince of Wales Gate
Knightsbridge Barracks
Alexandra Gate
A315
Queens Gate
Knightsbridge
Kensington road
Kensington gore
Albert Hall mans
Exhibition road
Queens gate
ROYAL ALBERT HALL
Royal College of Art
Prince Consort rd
Prince's gate
Prince's gdns
Montrose ct
Moncorvo cl
Ennismore Gardens
Rutland ga
Rutland gdns
Montpelier sq
Trevor pl
Hyde Park gate
Palace ga
De Vere gdns
Victoria rd
Canning pl
Kensington ga

A B C D E F G H J K L M

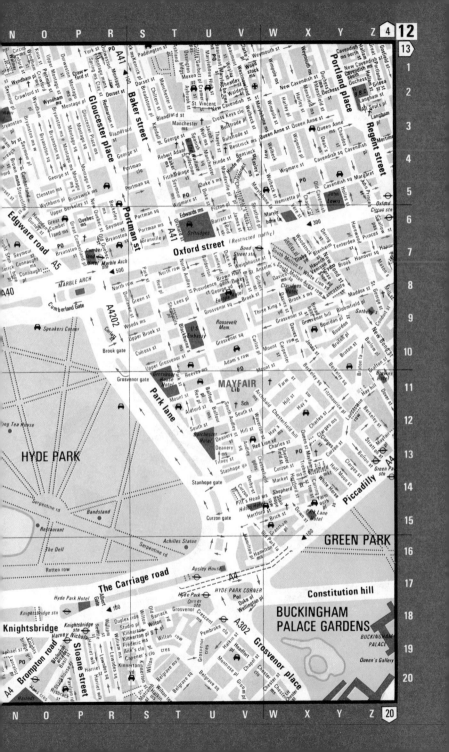

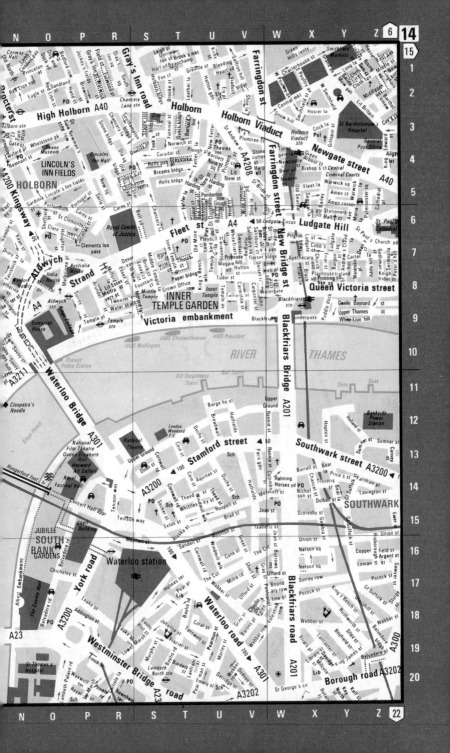

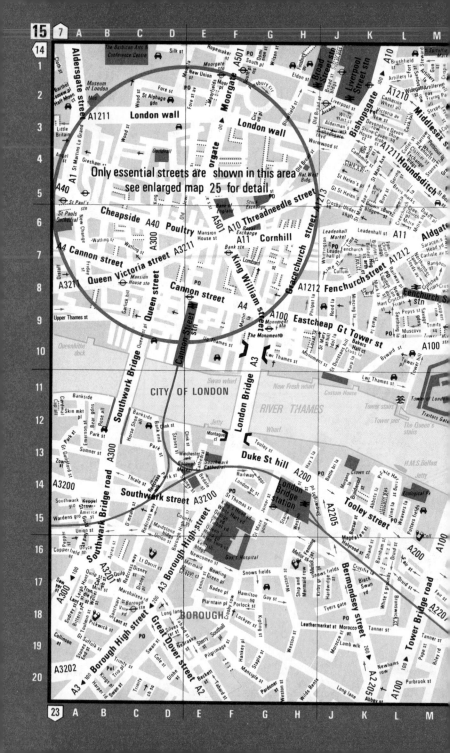

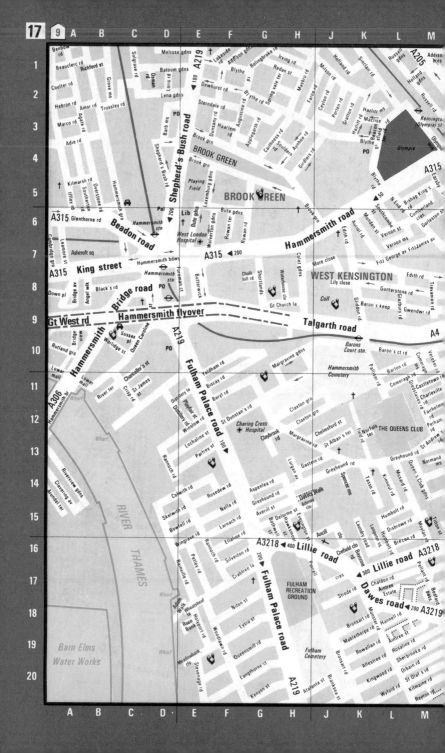

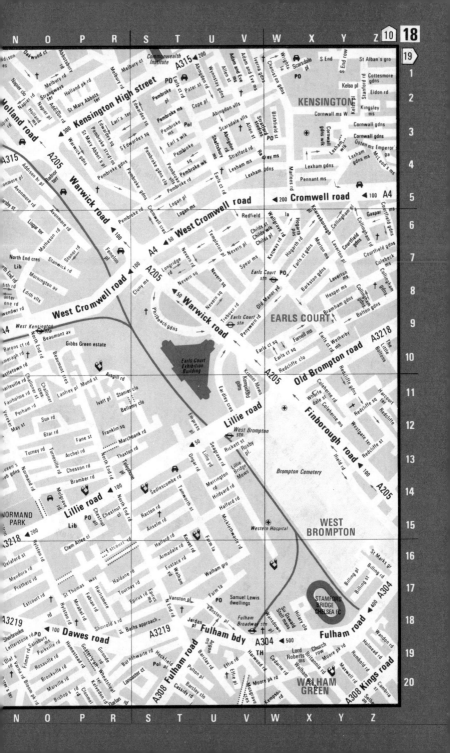

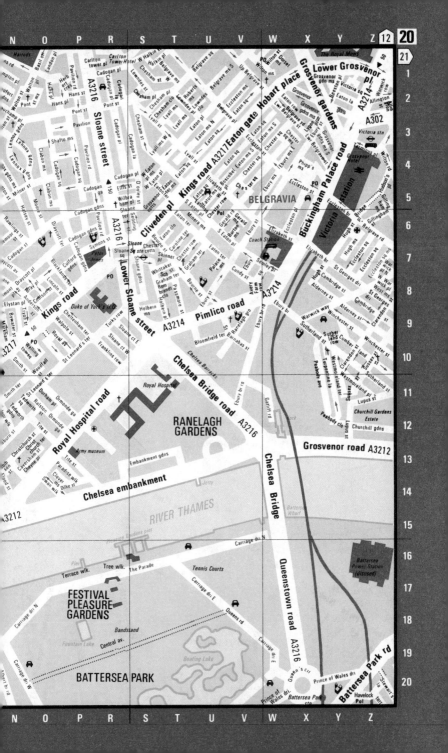

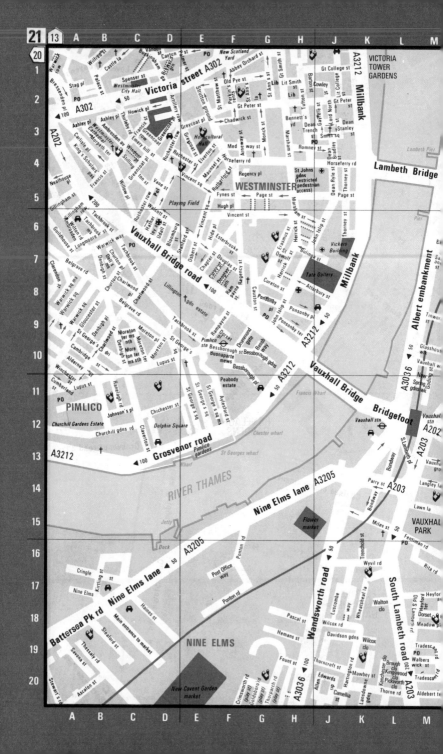

BERMONDSEY

SOUTHWARK PARK

1
2
3
4
5
6
7
8
9
10
11
12
13
14
15
16
17
18
19
20

Maltby st · Neckinger · Enid st · Old Jamaica rd · New Place sq · Slippers pl

Grange wlk · Grange yd · Town Hall · Lib · Spa rd · West · Spa rd · Thurland rd · Dockley rd · St James's rd · Ben Smith way · John Roll way · Tranton rd · Keeton's rd · Lockwood sq

Grange road · Keyse rd · Dunlop pl · Dockley rd · Lucey rd · Webster rd · Stork's rd · Clement's rd · Southwark Pk rd · Stalham st

Kintore st · Alscot rd · Vauban st · Bowel rd · Eveline Lowe · Rouel rd · Alexis st · Blue Anchor la · Bombax rd · Banyard rd · Wat dale clo

Grange road · Alma gro · Macks rd · St James's rd · Layard sq · Layard rd · Southwark Pk rd · Culmington rd · Asquinden rd · Abbeyfield rd · Masing ton rd · Neilldale rd · Ped worth

Alscot rd · Duntan st · Balaclava rd · 50 · Southwark Park road · 200 · 300 · Raymouth road · A2206

Lynton rd · Fort rd · Reverdy rd · Longley rd · Monnow rd · PO · Trothy rd · St James's rd · Beatrice rd · Camilla rd · Amicable · Anchor st · Raberry st · Almond rd · Galley Wall road · A2208 · 200

Alma gro · Reverdy rd · Thorburn sq · Strathnairn st · Simms rd · Beatrice rd · Camilla rd · Linda st · Lynton rd

Earl cotts · Lynton rd · Welstford st · Esmeralda rd · Lynton rd · Hyson rd

Earl rd · Hamilton sq · Burgandy st · Row cross pl · Alderminster rd · Rolls rd · St James's rd · Catlin st · Ilderton rd · Credon rd · Cranswick rd · Bramcote gro · Dela ford rd · Boxn · Ablett st

A2 · Coburg rd · Oakley pl · Colyers · Mawbey pl · Brodie st · Longland ct · Egan way · Starleigh way · Barkworth rd

Nile ter · Trafalgar av · Glengall rd · Old Kent road · Avondale sq · Marborough gro · Lovegrove st · St James's rd · Fenham · Tenterden · Leonard · Marwood · Lynstead · Radnor · Redlaw way · Verney way · Verney rd · Boythorn way · Varcoe rd

Waite st · Glengall ter · Ossory rd · Malt st · PO · A2208 · St James's rd · Verney rd · Sandgate st · Ruby triangle

Recreation ground · Neate st · Bowyers rd · Radley st · Canal gro · Sandgate st · Ruby st · Gas works

St George's way · Olma st · Frens ham st · Peckham Pk rd · Shard's · Lib · Livesey pl · pl · Lib · Hyndman st · Ruby st · Murdock st · Devon st

Cator st · Davey st · Bianca rd · Latona rd · Maismore st · Green Hundred rd · Etthard · Pencraig · 700 · Old Kent road · Devonshire gro · Sylvan gro

Alder clo · Daniel gdns · Summer rd · Colegrove rd · Unwin rd · Peckham Pk rd · Commercial way · Asylum rd · Drover la · A2

Garnies clo · Willowbrook rd · Reddins rd · Bird-in-Bush rd · Bird-in-Bush rd · Friary rd · Ledbury st · Gervase st · Leo st · Clifton cres

Nutt st · Radnor rd · Limpston Gdn est · Hoyland clo · Naler rd · Nutcroft rd · Clifton cres

G.L.C. Housing Estate · Rosemary rd · Commercial way · Farley rd · Elcot av · Holbeck row · Studholme st · Sprin · Culmore rd

Jowett st · Peckham Hill st · Hastings clo · Leontine clo · Elcot av · Fenham rd · Pennethorne rd · Blanch clo · Clifton way

Cator st · East Surrey gro · Commercial way · Sumner rd · Buller clo · Wilmot clo · Wentworth cres · Farley rd · Marmont rd · Friary rd · Kincaid rd · Meeting House la · Carlton gro · Montpelier · King's gro · Asylum rd · Laburnam clo

Camden · Sumner rd · Bonar rd

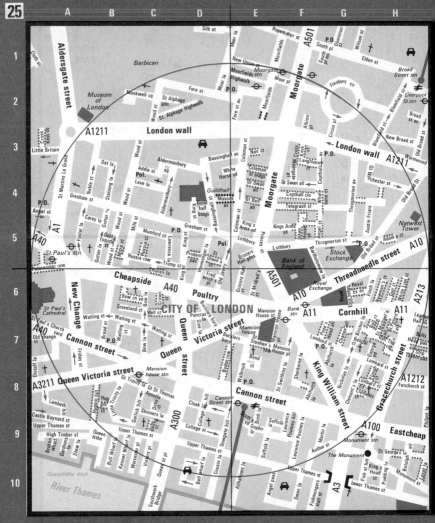

Enlargement of crowded city area for extra clarity

ROYAL LONDON GUIDE

ROYAL LONDON GUIDE

London is rich in royal connections. Since 1066 every British monarch has been crowned at Westminster Abbey and has maintained a royal residence in the capital or just outside, along the banks of the River Thames.

The hundreds of years of royal influence have left their mark not only in palaces and churches, but in Royal Parks and foundations, statues, memorials and even streets. History has not stopped, however. The Royal Family are still largely based in London and Windsor; they marry in London, shop in London, attend ceremonies in London, and anyone prepared to stand on the right pavement at the appropriate time may see the Queen herself, and members of her family, pass by in car or carriage.

EVENTS & CEREMONIES

London is famous for royal and military pageantry, which frequently amounts to free street theatre, some of it backed by excellent military bands. Probably the most famous event is Changing the Guard at Buckingham Palace; the most spectacular – Trooping the Colour; the most theatrical – the Royal Tournament; the oldest – the Ceremony of the Keys at the Tower of London; the most obscure – the Quit Rent Ceremony at the Royal Courts of Justice. In a few cases tickets must be applied for well in advance, but much may be enjoyed by anyone willing to stand on the right pavement at the right time. *The Times*, *The Daily Telegraph* and *The Independent* all publish a Court Circular listing the Royal Family's various public engagements. The following are regular daily or annual events.

Daily ceremonies

CHANGING THE GUARD

The ceremonial guards outside Buckingham Palace, St James's Palace, at Horse Guards and Windsor Castle change at regular times, following a time-honoured drill. All are major tourist attractions.

Buckingham Palace   *13 A 18*
SW1. Changing the Guard takes place inside the palace railings, and in summer the crowd makes it hard to see much. An alternative is to watch the guards on their way from Chelsea or Wellington Barracks; telephone the London Tourist Board Information Centre (01-730 3488) to find out which location they are leaving from on a particular day. Guards leave *Chelsea Barracks at 10.45, or Wellington Barracks at 11.00. Palace ceremony 11.30 Mon–Sun in summer, alternate days in winter.*

St James's Palace   *13 C 15*
SW1. A detachment of the Buckingham Palace Guard comes here. Guards change *11.15 Mon–Sun in summer, alternate days in winter.*

Horse Guards   *13 H 15*
Whitehall SW1. This is the scene of the Changing of the Queen's Life Guard, mounted on splendid black horses. Guards leave *Knightsbridge Barracks 10.38 Mon–Sat, 09.39 Sun. Ceremony at 11.00 Mon–Sat, 10.00 Sun.*

Windsor Castle
Windsor, Berks. The Queen's out of town and favoured residence. The Guard changes *Mon–Sat at 10.30.* A military band enlivens the pageant.

CEREMONY OF THE KEYS

Tower of London   *15 M 11*
Tower Hill EC3. 01-709 0765. The Chief Warder of the Yeomen Warders of the Tower, with an escort of the Brigade of Guards, locks the West Gates, the Middle Tower and Byward Tower. One of the oldest continuous military ceremonies in the world. *Takes place Mon–Sun 21.40.* Apply in writing for tickets to the Governor of the Tower, enclosing a stamped addressed envelope, well in advance.

Annual events & ceremonies

JANUARY

Royal Epiphany Gifts   *13 D 15*
Chapel Royal, St James's Palace SW1. Picturesque ceremony when two Gentlemen Ushers offer gifts of gold, frankincense and myrrh on behalf of the Queen. Admission

by ticket only – apply in writing to the Lord Chamberlain's Office, St James's Palace SW1. *Ceremony at 11.30 on 6th Jan.*

King Charles I Memorial Service   13   J   15

Banqueting House, Whitehall SW1. 01-930 4179. Charles I, the last English monarch to be beheaded, stepped on to a scaffold from a window of the Banqueting House on 30th January 1649. On the anniversary, the hall becomes a chapel for the sake of a service in honour of the king, held by the Society of King Charles the Martyr. *Service at 11.30 on 30th Jan.*

King Charles I Memorial Service   13   H   12

Trafalgar Sq WC2. A service and wreath-laying in honour of the king takes place at his statue in Trafalgar Square annually. This one is organised by The Royal Stuart Society. *Service at 11.00 on 30th Jan.*

MARCH

Royal Film Performance   13   H   10

Odeon, Leicester Sq WC2. 01-930 6111. A selected film gets royal patronage in aid of The Cinema and Television Benevolent Fund. It is attended on alternate years by the Queen and the Queen Mother, who are both patrons of the charity. If the idea of joining the crowds to watch the royal and celebrity arrivals is too daunting, bear in mind that the event is well covered on television. *No fixed date.*

JUNE

Trooping the Colour   13   H   15

Horse Guards Parade, Whitehall SW1. On this, the Queen's Official Birthday, the colour of one of the five regiments of Foot Guards – the Grenadiers, Coldstream, Scots, Irish or Welsh – is ceremonially trooped before the Queen, who takes the salute.

Until 1986 Her Majesty attended on horseback, wearing the uniform of Colonel in Chief of whichever of the five regiments was on parade. But her mount, Burmese, was officially retired in that year, and since 1987 she has ridden to the ceremony in a carriage.

Those hoping for tickets to the event or to

one of the full-scale dress rehearsals should apply in writing, with a stamped addressed envelope, to the Brigade Major, Household Division, Horse Guards, Whitehall, SW1, between 1st Jan and 1st Mar. Tickets are awarded by ballot. Unlucky applicants can still enjoy some of London's best pageantry by lining the processional route from Buckingham Palace, along The Mall, to Horse Guards Parade. *Held on 11th Jun or nearest Sat.*

Founder's Day   20   P   10

Royal Hospital, Royal Hospital Rd, Chelsea SW3. 01-730 0161. The founder of this hospital for aged or disabled soldiers was Charles II, and on this day his statue in the courtyard is garlanded with oak leaves, in memory of his escape from the Round-heads when he hid in an oak tree. The Chelsea Pensioners parade for inspection, sometimes by royalty. Also known as Oak Apple Day. *Early Jun.*

Garter Ceremony

St George's Chapel, Windsor Castle, Windsor, Berks. (0753) 868286. The annual Garter Service is held just before Royal Ascot. The Queen invests new Knights of the Order in the throne room at the castle. There is then a spectacular procession from the Upper Ward of the Castle to the Chapel, attended by heralds, made up of the Queen and members of the Royal Family in Garter Robes, Knights of the Garter and others. The public may watch from within the castle precincts. After the service, the procession returns the way it came. *3rd week in Jun.*

Royal Ascot Races

Ascot Racecourse, near Windsor, Berks. A one-week race meeting which is also a fashionable society event. Many men wear morning suits, women attire formally in dresses and hats – in fact the hats sometimes attract as much attention as the horses. It is possible to apply for tickets to the Royal Enclosure (see the Court pages of *The Times*; *The Daily Telegraph* or *The Independent* in December for instructions), but tickets are limited and it is necessary to find a sponsor who has attended on at least four occasions or is known personally to the Queen. *Mid Jun.*

JULY

Royal Tournament March Past   13   H   15

Horse Guards, Whitehall SW1. Colourful parade of all troops taking part in the Royal Tournament. *Sun before the Tournament itself.*

Royal Tournament   18   T   10

Earl's Court, Warwick Rd SW5. 01-371 8141. Impressive military event with marching displays, massed military bands, the famous musical ride of the Royal Artillery, and spectacular lighting and theatrical effects. Tickets bookable at Earl's Court box office. Lasts for two weeks. *Mid-Jul.*

Burmese
Perhaps the most famous ceremonial horse. She was ridden by the Queen at Trooping the Colour from 1969 until 1986 when the elegant black mare, still spry, retired at the age of 24. Her loss has changed the face of history – the Queen now attends the ceremony in a carriage.

OCTOBER

Quit Rent Ceremony　　**14　R　6**
Royal Courts of Justice, Strand WC2. 01-405 7641. Ceremony in which the City Solicitor pays a token rent of two faggots of wood, a billhook and a hatchet for a piece of land in Shropshire, and six horseshoes and 61 nails for a forge in the Strand which no longer exists. The Queen's Remembrancer is on the receiving end of this archaic piece of pantomime. Apply for tickets to the Chief Clerk to the Queen's Remembrancer, Room 118, Royal Courts of Justice, Strand WC2. *Late Oct.*

NOVEMBER

State Opening of Parliament　**13　K　20**
Houses of Parliament, St Margaret St SW1. The Queen, in the Irish State Coach, is driven from Buckingham Palace to the House of Lords. A Royal Salute is fired in Hyde Park and at the Tower of London. The formal ceremony, during which the Queen reads a speech outlining the proposed legislation of the Government for the new session of Parliament, is not open to the public, but is televised. However it is possible to apply to the Lord Great Chamberlain's Office at the House of Lords, SW1, for a pavement ticket. Only a few are available but those in possession have a good view of the arrival of the royal party. Otherwise it is worth finding a place along the processional route. *Early Nov.*

British Legion Festival　　**11　E　19**
of Remembrance
Royal Albert Hall, Kensington Gore SW7. 01-589 8212. Held on the Saturday evening before the remembrance service at the Cenotaph and well attended by the Royal Family. A moving sight as thousands of poppies cascade to the floor. *Sat nearest 11th Nov.*

Remembrance Day Service　**13　J　17**
The Cenotaph, Whitehall SW1. The service, to remember the dead of two world wars, is held at the Cenotaph and attended by the Queen, members of the Royal Family, leading politicians, and representatives of the armed and support services. A salute is fired, two minutes' silence observed, wreaths of poppies laid on Lutyens' famous memorial, and a march past undertaken by current and ex-servicemen and women. *Sun nearest 11th Nov.*

Royal Command Variety　　**14　N　8**
Performance
Theatre Royal Drury Lane, Catherine St WC2. 01-836 8108. Lavish big-name variety show in aid of the Variety Artists Benevolent Fund, attended alternate years by the Queen and the Queen Mother, who are both patrons of the charity. Crowds collect on the pavement to watch the audience arrive. The royal and celebrity arrivals, and extensive extracts from the show, are televised. *No fixed date.*

Royal Salutes

Hyde Park W2　　　　　　　**12　P　16**
Tower of London EC3　　　　**15　M　11**
On certain significant occasions or anniversaries a royal salute of 41 guns is fired in Hyde Park and of 62 guns at the Tower of London, always at *12.00* (noon). These salutes are fired on the actual dates given below except when the date falls on a Sunday in which case the salute is fired at *12.00* on the following day. The Prince of Wales does not get a salute on his birthday, although flags are flown.

6th February
The anniversary of the accession to the throne of Queen Elizabeth II.
21st April
The occasion of the Queen's actual birthday (as distinct from her Official Birthday in June).
2nd June
The anniversary of the Queen's Coronation in 1953.
10th June
The birthday of the Duke of Edinburgh.
11th June
The Queen's Official Birthday and the occasion of Trooping the Colour.
4th August
The birthday of Queen Elizabeth, the Queen Mother.
Early November
The occasion of the State Opening of Parliament.

By Invitation Only

ROYAL GARDEN PARTIES
Buckingham Palace　　　**12　X　18**
SW1. A select few (although their numbers may seem large to passers-by watching the arrival of sleek cars, top hats and flowered creations) enjoy strawberries and cream in a marquee on the lawns behind Buckingham Palace. The parties are always extremely well attended by members of the Royal Family, who mingle with their guests throughout the afternoon. There are three such parties a year. *Each is held mid-week, during the month of Jul.*

INVESTITURES
Buckingham Palace　　　**13　A　18**
SW1. These are the occasions upon which the Queen presents orders, decorations and medals in the ballroom of the palace. Recipients are usually allowed two guests. There are approximately 14 investitures a year, *held at 11.00 (usually six in the spring, two in Jul and six more between Oct and Dec).*

PALACES, CASTLES & ROYAL RESIDENCES

Several of the Royal Palaces in or near London are open to the public, including three which visitors don't always regard as such – The Tower of London, The Palace of Westminster and Windsor Castle. The most famous – Buckingham Palace – is not open to the public, though the ceremony of Changing the Guard and the possibility of seeing the Royal Family coming and going draws the crowds. Little remains of the once great palaces of Greenwich, Richmond and Whitehall, but they were so important in their day that their sites still have the power to attract.

Buckingham Palace   **13 A 18**
SW1. 01-930 4832. The London residence of the Sovereign – the Royal Standard flying on the roof indicates that she is at home. Apart from the Queen's Gallery and the Royal Mews, it is not practical to admit the public since much of the building is in fact an office complex. All the private secretaries and relevant offices of the Queen, the Duke of Edinburgh, the Prince and Princess of Wales, Princess Anne, the Duke and Duchess of York and Prince Edward are situated here, as are the offices of the Master of the Household and the Master of the Privy Purse and, indeed, the Press Office. No wonder the Duke of Edinburgh made his famous remark about 'living above the shop'.

Originally built in 1705 as the Duke of Buckingham's House, it was remodelled into a palace by Nash in 1830 and refaced by Sir Aston Webb in 1913. Its 40 acres of grounds and gardens, a haven for wild birds, are the setting for prestigious summer garden parties, by invitation only. The military pomp and pageantry of Changing the Guard *starts daily at 11.30 (alternate days in winter)*. The central first floor balcony is traditionally used by the Queen and other members of the Royal Family as a vantage point from which to wave to the public on or after ceremonial occasions – a royal wedding, for example, or Trooping the Colour. *Not open to the public.*

Clarence House   **13 B 16**
Stable Yard Rd SW1. The London residence of the Queen Mother since 1953, it was rebuilt by John Nash in 1828 for the then Duke of Clarence, later William IV. Apart from the last three years of the Second World War, when it was the HQ of both the Red Cross and the St John's Ambulance Brigade, the house has always been a royal residence. The present Queen lived here when she was Princess Elizabeth; it was the birthplace of Princess Anne, and the list of previous royal tenants includes George

III's daughter Princess Augusta, Queen Victoria's mother the Duchess of Kent, and her son the Duke of Connaught. On Queen Elizabeth the Queen Mother's Birthday, 4th August, a lone piper plays on the lawn outside. *Not open to the public.*

Eltham Palace
Off Court Yard, Eltham SE9. 01-859 2112. Once a Royal Palace, beloved of kings from Henry III to Henry VIII. Henry IV was married here – although his bride, Joan of Navarre, was not present at the time since it was a proxy affair. Rebuilding in the 1930s and the fact that it is now the HQ of the Directorate of Army Education, has somewhat changed the atmosphere, but the restored Banqueting Hall with its hammerbeam roof and oriel windows is splendid – and is open to the public. *Open 11.00–16.00 Thur & Sun in winter; 11.00–17.00 Thur & Sun in summer. Closed Mon–Wed, Fri & Sat.* Free.

Greenwich Palace
Greenwich Park SE10. The palace no longer exists, but the beautiful Wren buildings that make up the Royal Naval College stand on its site. During the time of the Tudors it was reportedly a fine structure, extended and rebuilt over the years, and – as can still be understood today – on a magical riverside site.

Henry VI, Henry VII and Henry VIII lived here, and so did Elizabeth I and James I, for whose Queen the still-surviving Queen's House (central portion of the National Maritime Museum) was built by Inigo Jones. Charles II rebuilt part of the palace, but William and Mary eschewed it, the nearby river being thought unsuitable for William's asthma. Shortly after this it was finally demolished.

The palace was the setting for several important royal events – Henry VIII, Mary I and Elizabeth I were born here; Prince Arthur married Catherine of Aragon and Henry VIII was married by proxy to Anne of Cleves; Catherine of Aragon was imprisoned here for two years. Here, too, were signed the death warrants of Anne Boleyn and Mary Queen of Scots.

Hampton Court Palace
Hampton Court, Middx. 01-977 8441. Built by Cardinal Wolsey from 1514 and given to Henry VIII in 1529 in an unsuccessful attempt to regain favour. Enlarged by Henry VIII, repaired by Charles II, extended under William and Mary by Christopher Wren, with further interior decoration carried out on the orders of Queen Anne, George I and George II. It is vast, grand, on a prime riverside site, with a collection of Italian masterpieces among other important paintings (though these are sometimes on loan

to other exhibitions). Its grounds, which contain the famous Maze, are sweeping, varied and beautiful.

The State Apartments were first opened to the public by Queen Victoria and are extensive, with elaborate ceiling paintings, wide window views, tapestries, pictures and some original furniture; they include the Chapel Royal, approached by the Haunted Gallery along which the doomed Catherine Howard ran in a vain attempt to plead with the praying king, Henry VIII, for her life; the impressive Great Watching Chamber and the Great Hall with its superb hammerbeam roof.

A fire in 1986 destroyed one of the Grace and Favour apartments and damaged part of the State Apartments, which are closed for restoration work, but there is still plenty to see. Don't miss the less obvious entrances to the Renaissance Picture Gallery, the buttery, wine cellars and Great Kitchens. *Open 09.30–18.00 Mon–Sun Apr–Sep (to 17.00 Oct–Mar). Closed winter Nat Hols.* Charge.

Kensington Palace　　　　**10　Y　15**
Kensington Gardens W8. 01-937 9561. The former Nottingham House was rebuilt by Wren for William III and extended and redecorated by William Benson and William Kent for George I. It was the principal residence of the Sovereign until the death of George II in 1760. Queen Victoria and George V's Queen, Mary of Teck, were both born here and it was here on 20th June 1837 that the young Victoria was told she had become Queen. Later, her daughter Princess Louise, who sculpted the statue of Victoria which stands outside the palace, lived here. Other royal events at Kensington Palace have included the quarrel of the Duchess of Marlborough with Queen Anne, the death of Queen Anne and later of George II. Kensington remains royal – the Dowager Princess Alice, the Prince and Princess of Wales, Princess Margaret, the Duke and Duchess of Gloucester and Prince and Princess Michael of Kent all have apartments here.

Standing to one side of the lovely Kensington Gardens, this remains one of the most charming and least awe-inspiring of palaces. Even the sumptuous State Apartments, the only part open to the public, seem compact and accessible. The visitor will find portraits, furniture and tapestries, Victoria's bedroom, full of mementoes, with her dolls' house and toys nearby; a museum of artefacts shown at the Great Exhibition; the circular cupola room; and the Court Dress collection. *Open 09.00–17.00 Mon–Sat; 13.00–17.00 Sun. Closed some Nat Hols.* Charge.

Kew Palace
Kew Gardens, Richmond, Surrey. 01-940 7333. The Dutch House, as it is sometimes called, was built in 1631 for a merchant called Samuel Fortrey. In 1802 George III

and Queen Charlotte used it while they awaited the building of a new summer palace, which was never completed. The Queen in particular loved the chunky brick house – and died here in 1818. It is set to one side of the 300 acres of the Royal Botanic Gardens, which are well worth exploring.

The house contains an impressive needlework picture of George III, portraits of the King and Queen by Zoffery, the King's own dressing table, and the chair in which the Queen is said to have died. The Pages' Waiting Room has an exhibition of royal knick-knacks, including a heavy silver rattle fit to brain a baby, and an illustrated family tree from George I to Queen Victoria. The Library has limited books but a case full of George IV's fishing tackle. *Open Apr–Sep 11.00–17.30 Mon–Sun. Closed Oct–Mar, Good Fri & May Day.* Charge.

Lancaster House　　　　**13　B　16**
Stable Yard, St James's SW1. Begun by Smirke in 1820 for the Grand Old Duke of York (but George IV quarrelled with the architect and forced his brother to appoint Wyatt in his place), and known at first as York House. When it was acquired by the first Duke of Sutherland, formerly Marquess of Stafford, it was renamed Stafford House. In 1912 the first Viscount Leverhulme bought it for the nation and named it after his home county. Its decorous town-house exterior is no real preparation for the truly luscious Baroque splendours of its interior. This, and the fact that it is now used as a government and state hospitality centre gives it the air of a fine hotel of the old school.

The centrepiece is Sir Charles Barry's magnificent staircase. On the flamboyantly decorative upper floor there are ceiling paintings by H. Howard RA and by Veronese and the sumptuous Great Gallery has a ceiling painting of *St Crisoganus Borne To Heaven By Angels*, which was brought here from a church in Rome.

Queen Victoria was a frequent guest in the days of the 2nd Duke of Sutherland, whose wife was Mistress of the Robes, and the Queen and Prince Albert enjoyed a recital by Chopin here. This was also the setting, in 1953, of Elizabeth II's coronation banquet. *Open 14.00–18.00 Sat, Sun & Nat Hols only, between Easter & mid-Dec. Closed at short notice for functions.* Free.

Marlborough House　　　　**13　D　15**
Marlborough Gate, Pall Mall SW1. 01-930 8071. Charming 18thC red brick Wren building, added to by Pennington in the 19thC, which was built for Sarah, first Duchess of Marlborough, and is now the Commonwealth Centre. It contains a painted ceiling by Gentileschi which was originally designed for the Queen's House at Greenwich. The two-storey-high salon has wall paintings by Louis Laguerre depicting the Battle of Blenheim, and more of his paintings decorate the staircase walls.

Among its illustrious tenants were Edward, Prince of Wales, later Edward VII; George V, who was born here and lived here as Prince of Wales; Queen Alexandra who spent her widowhood here and whose memorial is in Marlborough Road; and George V's widow, Queen Mary, who died here in 1953. *Tours at 11.00 & 15.00 Mon–Fri, by telephone application to the Administration Officer.* Charge.

Palace of Westminster   *13 K 20*
St Margaret St SW1. 01-219 3000. The building known as the Houses of Parliament is in fact the New Palace of Westminster, by Barry and Pugin, 1840–68. Part of it, the House of Commons, was damaged by Second World War incendiary bombs and rebuilt to a simpler design by Sir Giles Gilbert Scott between 1945–50. It is a grand and glorious Gothic structure built around the late 11thC Westminster Hall whose 14thC timber roof rivals any in Europe. Still has Royal Palace status.

The Old Palace of Westminster was built for Edward the Confessor and remained the Sovereign's chief residence in London until Henry VIII moved the Court to Whitehall Palace in 1512. It included the Royal Chapel of St Stephen which ceased to be a chapel at the Reformation and became the meeting place of the House of Commons. This accounts for the arrangement of the British Parliament – the opposing parties facing each other as though still in the original choir stalls, with the Speaker where the altar would have been. Apart from this and Westminster Hall the only other survivor of the original palace is the Jewel Tower, once Edward III's treasure house, now displaying medieval carvings and 11thC capitals from Westminster Hall.

Visitors may tour the building when the House is not sitting (or listen to debates from the Strangers' Gallery when it is); they will see the Commons, the older and more gorgeous red and gold House of Lords, various ante rooms and galleries and the Royal Robing Rooms where the Queen and the Duke of Edinburgh prepare for the official Opening of Parliament. There are sometimes optional extra tours up St Stephen's Tower and behind the four faces of the clock known as Big Ben – though in fact the name belongs to the bell, cast at Whitechapel in 1858, whose hourly chimes are broadcast to the nation. *Open Mon–Sat to limited numbers.* Write to your MP for an invitation or join the queue outside (the duty policemen will advise on your chances of getting in that day). Free.

Palace of Whitehall   *13 J 14*
Whitehall SW1. 01-930 4179. This palace was the principal London residence of the Court during the 15th and 16th centuries. New plans for it were drawn up during the reign of James I, and the Banqueting House, built by Inigo Jones, was added to the original palace in 1625. This splendid piece of architecture was the first Palladian building to be completed in England. Being largely built of timber, the palace was destroyed by two fires in 1691 and 1698, leaving only the more recent stone-built Banqueting House still standing. Today, when it is not in use for government functions, the public may enter this gracious and spacious hall and admire the nine allegorical ceiling paintings designed for Charles I by Peter Paul Rubens. His reward on their completion in 1629 included a knighthood. The central oval shows the *Apotheosis of James I*, and the picture on the north side of the hall the birth and coronation of Charles himself.

The weathercock is reputed to have been set up by James II to indicate whether or not the wind was likely to blow the Prince of Orange across the seas. A tablet marks the window where Charles I stepped out to his execution. The hall once saw service as a Royal Chapel and returns to this role each 30th January for a commemoration service in honour of the beheaded monarch. *Open 10.00–17.00 Tue–Sat; 14.00–17.00 Sun. Closed Mon (except Nat Hols) & when in use.* Charge.

Richmond Palace
Richmond, Surrey. At the north-west corner of Richmond Green stands an old gateway on which the arms of Henry VII can just be recognised. This, and the Wardrobe buildings tucked away in Old Palace Yard, are all that remains of a once great palace begun in 1510 to replace the earlier Palace of Shene. Henry VII died here, Anne of Cleves lived in it after her divorce from Henry VIII, Edward VI stayed in it frequently, Mary and Philip of Spain honeymooned in it, Elizabeth I spent summers here late in her reign, and Charles I used it as a hunting lodge. At his execution the palace was mostly destroyed; and although it was partly repaired at the Restoration, and James II had ideas of refurbishing it, it never recovered and the rest was destroyed, or collapsed, piecemeal.

St James's Palace   *13 B 15*
Pall Mall SW1. The Tudor gatehouse, in warm red brick with blue diapering, gives on to courtyards and buildings planned for Henry VIII, but with important later additions and reconstructions. This palace is still officially a royal residence and foreign Ambassadors and High Commissioners are still accredited to the Court of St James, though they are received at Buckingham Palace. Like Buckingham Palace, St James's is not open to the public – who may do no more than watch the Changing of the Guard outside – and like Buckingham Palace it contains offices. The offices of the Lord Chamberlain's Department are here and so are residences for some of the officials of the Royal Household.

It became the principal London residence of the Sovereign after the destruction of Whitehall Palace. Elizabeth I and James I held Court here. Charles I left from here for his execution, and Charles II lived here and enjoyed the nearby St James's Park, which he extended. Queen Anne, George I, George II and George III spent much of their London-based time here. Royalty ceased to live at the palace early in the 19thC but it still saw important events; Queen Victoria was married here and so was George V. *Not open to the public.*

The Ravens
The presence of the ravens at the Tower of London is traditional, and legend says the Tower will fall if they leave and England will lose its greatness; against which awesome eventuality their wings are clipped. There are six of them – with a 41p per day official allowance for their meat ration – under the care of a Yeoman Ravenmaster, one of the Yeomen Warders. Their heavy blackness, flopping movements, vicious beaks and grating croaks make them suitably unpleasant companions for the memories and instruments of death and torture within these grim walls.

The Tower of London   15 M 10
Tower Hill EC3. 01-709 0765. This grim and famous fortress looks deceptively pale and innocent from outside. Red-clad Yeomen Warders and black ravens guard the Bloody Tower, the Traitor's Gate, the armouries, the executioner's block and axe and, of course, the Crown Jewels.

It was begun by William the Conqueror – the White Tower, or keep, is his – and has been added to by many of the sovereigns who followed. It has been one of the most impregnable fortresses in England, an arsenal and a prison.

It is still designated a Royal Palace and was also a royal residence until the time of James I. It has housed the Royal Mint, the Public Records, the Royal Observatory and the Royal Menagerie.

Among the many imprisoned within it have been the young Princess Elizabeth, Sir Walter Raleigh, Roger Casement and Rudolf Hess. Those beheaded on its green include Anne Boleyn, Catherine Howard and the 17-year-old Lady Jane Grey. Many more were taken from it to public execution on Tower Hill.

It is possible to walk almost all around the curtain wall of the inner ward, taking in the Wakefield, Salt, Broad Arrow and Flint Towers and also the Martin Tower from which Colonel Blood tried to steal the Crown Jewels in 1671.

There are two chapels – the Chapel Royal of St Peter Ad Vincula and the Norman Chapel of St John and the whole edifice is London's oldest and most popular museum. *Open 09.30–17.00 Mon–Sat (16.00 in winter); 14.00–17.00 Sun. Closed Sun winter & Nat Hols.* Charge.

Windsor Castle
Windsor, Berks. (0753) 868286. Eight hundred-year-old medieval fortress, magnificently visible for miles around, adjoining nearly 5,000 acres of home park and gardens, most parts of which are open to the public and within which can be found Windsor Safari Park. Of all the Royal Palaces this is the one which has been occupied most consistently – the Queen is in official residence here for at least a quarter of the year, at Christmas, for parts of March, April and May and in June for Royal Ascot Week and the Garter Service in St George's Chapel.

The area covered by the castle is large, and time should be allowed to appreciate the walls, towers and gateways and the spectacularly scenic views, as well as the specific places of interest.

The public are admitted to St George's Chapel, the Chapel of the Order of the Garter, and into the State Apartments. The splendour of these rooms is rivalled by the many important paintings they contain. The Garter Throne Room has royal portraits; the Grand Reception Room has Gobelins tapestries; St George's Hall, which has more royal portraits, is the scene still of royal banquets; the Queen's Drawing Room has Van Dyck's portrait of Charles I's five eldest children and the King's Dressing Room has his famous triple picture of Charles I.

Also not to be missed are Queen Mary's Dolls' House, designed by Sir Edwin Lutyens, its pretend gardens laid out by Gertrude Jekyll; the Exhibition of Drawings from the Royal Collection; or the Royal Mews Exhibition which has equestrian paintings of the present Royal Family, as well as coaches and landaus. Because the castle is so much in royal use, opening times are complex.
Castle precinct open 10.00–sunset, Mon–Sun; closed Garter Day and state visit

The Corgis
The corgis, although they frequently travel the country with the Queen, are really town dogs (the labradors are based at Sandringham). There are currently five – and three 'dorgis'. The latter are the result of an unplanned romance between a corgi and one of Princess Margaret's dachshunds – and are not approved by the Kennel Club! Buckingham Palace says that 'As the Queen is not specifically mentioned in the relevant law, Her Majesty does not have dog licences.'

arrival day. State Apartments open 10.30–17.00 Mon–Sat, 13.30–17.00 Sun, May–Oct; 10.30–16.00 Mon–Sat, Nov–Apr; closed when Queen is in residence – usually 6 weeks at Easter, 3 weeks in Jun and 3 weeks at Christmas. Dolls' House, Draw- *ings and Royal Mews open 10.30–17.00 Mon–Sat, 13.30–17.00 Sun all year except New Year's day, Christmas day and Good Fri. St George's Chapel open 10.30–16.00 Mon–Sat, 13.30–16.00 Sun.* Charge (separate charge for each).

STATUES & MEMORIALS

Among London's numerous statues and memorials, many depict British kings and queens. Here is a selection of the best and most interesting.

Admiralty Arch   **13 H 13**
The Mall SW1. A massive memorial to Queen Victoria by Sir Aston Webb, erected astride The Mall in 1911.

Albert Memorial   **11 E 18**
Kensington Gardens SW7. A lavish Gothic monument to Queen Victoria's beloved consort; built by Sir George Gilbert Scott in 1863–72. The bronze of the prince sits under a canopy studying the catalogue to the Great Exhibition. The steps and podium seethe with the works of various sculptors, representing the continents, the arts and industry.

Prince Albert   **11 E 19**
Albert Hall, Kensington Gore SW7. On a column behind the Royal Albert Hall stands a bronze of Queen Victoria's consort by Joseph Durham, erected here in 1899.

Prince Albert   **14 U 3**
Holborn Circus EC1. Bronze equestrian statue by Charles Bacon, erected in 1874. Albert is raising his plumed hat, an unexpected gesture from a gentleman in uniform.

Queen Alexandra   **13 D 15**
Marlborough House, Marlborough Gate, Pall Mall SW1. The likeness of the wife of Edward VII was cast in bronze by Sir Alfred Gilbert and mounted on a plinth of red granite.

Queen Alexandra
London Hospital, Mile End Rd E1. A coronation bronze by George Edward Wade, erected here because the Queen presented the first phototherapy lamp to the hospital.

King Alfred   **15 C 20**
Trinity Church Sq SE1. London's oldest statue was moved here from Westminster Hall. Its weatherbeaten stone depicts a venerable kingly figure, strongly believed to be Alfred.

Queen Anne   **14 Z 6**
In front of St Paul's Cathedral, Ludgate Hill EC4. The original statue was erected in 1710, in honour of the fact that St Paul's was built during her reign; this marble copy was made in 1886.

Queen Anne   **13 F 19**
15 Queen Anne's Gate SW1. Early 18thC stone statue of the crowned Queen wearing the Order of the Garter. The unknown sculptor didn't quite finish off the back.

Queen Boadicea   **13 K 19**
Westminster Bridge SW1. More properly spelt Boudicca. Thomas Thornycroft's bronze, set up in 1902, shows the Queen of the Iceni driving her chariot horses as if by willpower – since he has given her no reins.

Buxton Memorial   **21 K 1**
Victoria Tower Gardens SW1. Anti-Slavery Party memorial by S. S. Teulon, erected in 1865. The crowned heads around it were replaced in fibreglass in 1980. They are Canute, Caractacus, Constantine, Alfred, William the Conqueror, Henry VII, Charles I and Queen Victoria.

Charles I   **13 J 14**
Banqueting House, Whitehall SW1. In a niche above the door of this remnant of the old Palace of Whitehall is a lead bust of the king, who stepped to his execution from this building.

Charles I   **13 H 20**
St Margaret's Church (East Door), Westminster, Parliament Sq SW1. Lead bust, sculptor unknown, found in Fulham in 1949 together with the one now at the Banqueting House.

Charles I   **13 H 12**
Trafalgar Sq SW1. Fine bronze equestrian statue cast by Hubert le Sueur in 1633 and notable for two things – it faces the site of the king's execution, and in 1655 Cromwell sold it to a brazier who said he had melted it down and sold relics of it to Royalists – however, it reappeared unharmed after the Restoration.

Charles II   **20 S 11**
Royal Hospital, Royal Hospital Rd, Chelsea SW3. The Grinling Gibbons bronze stands in the main courtyard of the Hospital for old soldiers which the king founded. It is garlanded on Oak Apple Day, the anniversary of his escape from the Roundheads, when he hid in an oak tree.

Charles II   **13 F 5**
Soho Sq SW1. Weathered stone statue sculpted by Caius Gabriel Cibber for this site, during Charles's reign. It was moved in the 19thC but restored here in 1938.

Edward I   **14**   **P**   **3**
National Westminster Bank, 114 High Holborn WC1. Look up at the outside of the building to see London's only statue of this king, sculpted in stone by Richard Garbe at the turn of the century.

Edward VI   **14**   **N**   **20**
St Thomas's Hospital, North Wing Terrace SW1. Here are two statues of the king who refounded the hospital,· one in stone with crown and sceptre by Thomas Cartwright in 1681, and one in bronze, with Garter Collar, by Peter Scheemakers in 1737.

Edward VII
Edward VII Memorial Park, Shadwell E1. The memorial, with its bronze medallion by Sir Bertram Mackenna, was unveiled by George V.

Edward VII   **14**   **P**   **3**
National Westminster Bank, 114 High Holborn WC1. High up on the building Edward VII, in stone by Richard Garbe, keeps company with Edward I.

Edward VII   **13**   **F**   **13**
Waterloo Pl SW1. Magnificent bronze equestrian statue on a Portland stone plinth by Sir Bertram Mackenna.

Eleanor Cross   **13**   **K**   **12**
Charing Cross Station, Strand WC2. An 1863 replica by E. M. Barry of the last of the 'Eleanor crosses' set up by Edward I to mark the resting places of his Queen's cortege on its route from Nottingham to Westminster Abbey.

Elizabeth I   **14**   **T**   **6**
St Dunstan-in-the-West, Fleet St EC4. The only known contemporary statue of her, in stone now much weathered, sculpted by William Kerwin in 1586.

George I   **13**   **J**   **3**
St George's Church, Bloomsbury Way WC1. Precariously placed atop the stepped pyramid steeple of Hawksmoor's church of 1730 and, oddly, enwrapped in a toga.

George II   **13**   **C**   **9**
Golden Sq W1. Contemporary lead statue, now painted white, by John Nost the Elder.

George II
Royal Naval College, Greenwich SW10. In the grand square of the College, which was formerly Greenwich Hospital, is a marble statue by J. M. Rysbrack, erected in 1735.

George III   **13**   **H**   **13**
Cockspur St SW1. Jaunty bronze equestrian statue, cast by Matthew Cotes Wyatt in 1836.

George IV   **13**   **H**   **12**
Trafalgar Sq SW1. Bronze equestrian statue by Sir Francis Legatt Chantrey, 1834. The king is sitting astride a calm horse.

George V   **13**   **J**   **20**
Old Palace Yard SW1. Wearing a Field Marshal's uniform and Garter Robes, the stone king was sculpted in 1947 by Sir William Reid Dick.

George VI   **13**   **F**   **14**
Carlton House Terrace SW1. Wearing the uniform of an Admiral of the Fleet and Garter Robes the statue by William Macmillan is at the top of the steps between Carlton House Terrace and The Mall.

Henry VIII   **14**   **Y**   **3**
St Bartholomew's Hospital EC1. A stone statue of 1702 by Francis Bird stands above the hospital gate.

James I   **13**   **J**   **14**
Banqueting House, Whitehall SW1. James I of England and VI of Scotland is commemorated by a bronze bust, commissioned by Charles I from Hubert le Sueur, and now inside the entrance hall. *Open 10.00–17.00 Tue–Sat; 14.00–17.00 Sun. Closed when in use for official functions. Charge.*

James II   **13**   **H**   **12**
Trafalgar Sq SW1. The bronze by Grinling Gibbons stands outside the National Gallery, on the opposite side of the entrance to the statue of Charles II.

Queen Mary   **13**   **D**   **15**
Marlborough House, Pall Mall SW1. The bronze medallion in the wall facing The Mall is by Sir William Reid Dick.

Mary Queen of Scots   **14**   **T**   **6**
143 Fleet St EC4. A stone statue by an unknown artist stands in a niche at first floor level.

Richard I   **13**   **K**   **20**
Houses of Parliament SW1. Romantic equestrian representation of the Lionheart by Baron Carlo Marochetti, 1860.

Temple Bar   **14**   **S**   **7**
Strand/Fleet St EC4. Monument by Sir Horace Jones, 1880, with marble figures of Queen Victoria and Edward, Prince of Wales by Sir Joseph Edgar Boehm.

Unknown Queen   **5**   **K**   **19**
Queen Sq WC1. The crowned and sceptred lead queen may be Charlotte, but no one knows for sure, nor who made her.

Queen Victoria   **13**   **F**   **14**
15 Carlton House Terrace SW1. Sculpted in marble by Sir Thomas Brock in 1897.

Queen Victoria   **21**   **D**   **1**
Caxton Hall, Caxton St SW1. A terracotta statue above the entrance, forms a pair with Edward VII.

Queen Victoria   **10**   **Z**   **15**
Kensington Gardens W2. White marble statue of the queen at the time of her succession to the throne; of special appeal because it was sculpted by her daughter, Princess Louise, in 1893.

Victoria Memorial   **13**   **A**   **17**
The Mall SW1. Dazzling white marble and gilded bronze allegorical group, designed by Sir Aston Webb, sculpted by Sir Thomas Brock and erected in 1911. Irreverently known as 'The Wedding Cake'. Good viewpoint for the changing of the guard at Buckingham Palace.

Westminster Old Boys'   **13**   **J**   **20**
Memorial
Westminster Abbey, Broad Sanctuary SW1. Red granite column by the west front, designed by Sir George Gilbert Scott in 1861, with small stone statues of Edward

the Confessor, Henry III, Elizabeth I and Victoria by J. R. Clayton.

William III **15 E 6**
Bank of England, Princes St EC2. The Bank, which was founded during his reign, has a stone statue by Sir Henry Cheere, carved in 1735, at the Princes Street entrance.

William III **10 Y 15**
Kensington Palace Gardens W8. Large bronze by H. Baucke, erected in 1907, outside the king's chosen residence.

William III **13 D 13**
St James's Sq SW1. Fine bronze equestrian statue by John Bacon and his son. Note the molehill which tripped the horse and caused the king to fall to his death – hence the Jacobite toast to 'the little gentleman in black velvet'.

William IV
William Walk, Greenwich SE10. The 'sailor king' is appropriately commemorated at Greenwich by a huge granite statue showing him in the uniform of Lord High Admiral, atop a tall 25ft-high granite pillar. The statue is by Samuel Nixon, the pillar by Richard Kelsey.

CHURCHES & CATHEDRALS

As the Queen is Defender of the Faith and Head of the Church of England, there is a sense in which all churches have a royal association. However, the churches and cathedrals included in this section are more royal than most.

Note: Chapel Royal is in fact the name of an institution rather than of a specific building which is why there are several of them. The medieval kings, who tended to keep their courts on the move, took the Chapel Royal with them. When the monarchy established the court in one place, the title settled on the Palace Chapel.

Chapel Royal
Hampton Court Palace, Hampton Court, Middx. 01-977 8441. The Chapel Royal at Hampton Court has a vaulted ceiling with gilded pendants, wall paintings and trompe l'oeil window by Thornhill and an elaborate oak reredos by Grinling Gibbons, all best viewed from the privileged position of the Royal Pew. This is reached by way of the chilly haunted gallery where Catherine Howard is said still to run screaming, hoping to plead for her life with Henry VIII, who remained inside at Mass, pretending not to hear her. Can be viewed as part of the tour of the palace. *Open to the public for Sun services at 08.30, 11.00 & 15.30, except during Aug.*

Chapel Royal **13 D 15**
St James's Palace SW1. Built in 1532 for Henry VIII, with a wonderfully coffered and painted ceiling which was renewed in the 18thC, and an aura of royal history. William and Mary, Queen Anne, George IV, Victoria and Albert, and George V and Mary of Teck were all married here. Less happily it was in this Chapel that Charles I took his last communion before his public execution. The Epiphany Gifts service takes place here – see under **Annual Events** for details. *Open to the public for regular Sun morning services from the 1st Sun in Oct to Good Fri.*

Chapel Royal **15 M 11**
HM Tower of London, Tower Hill EC3. The full title is the Chapel Royal of St Peter Ad Vincula. It is early 16thC, on even earlier foundations, and consecrated to 'The Festival of St Peter in Chains'. There are some illustrious, though unmarked, burials before the altar, of queens beheaded on nearby Tower Green – Anne Boleyn, Catherine Howard and the tragically young Lady Jane Grey. A Yeoman Warder will guide visitors around. *Open to the public for regular Sun morning services, apply at the Tower Gate.*

Chapel of St John **15 M 11**
HM Tower of London, Tower Hill EC3. Simple Norman Chapel, on the second floor of the White Tower, which is Britain's oldest church, still sanctified, and still commanding respect. Here Mary I was married by proxy to Philip of Spain.

Queen's Chapel **13 D 15**
Marlborough Rd SW1. By Inigo Jones, 1623–7. It was completed for Henrietta Maria, bride of Charles I, and refurbished for Catherine of Braganza when she married Charles II. George III married Queen Charlotte here. The beautiful panelling, coffered ceiling and Royal Pews may be admired by anyone attending Sunday morning service, though it has to be said that if too many people turn up it may not be possible to accommodate them all. *Open to the public for Sun morning service from Easter Sun to the last Sun in Jul.*

St George's Chapel
Windsor Castle, Windsor, Berks. St George's Chapel, which lies within the outer walls of the Castle, does not actually belong to the Crown but to the College of St George, a community of priests and laymen, who use admission charges to maintain the structure. Nevertheless it stands comparison with Westminster Abbey as a royal burial place. Here lie Edward IV, Henry VI, Henry VIII, Charles I, George III, George IV, William IV, Edward VII, George V and George VI.

The exceptionally beautiful late Gothic building was begun in 1475 by Edward IV, as a chapel for the Order of the Garter, founded by Edward III. It is the scene of the annual Garter Service in June – note the heraldic banners above the choir stalls and the Garter stall plates. *Open 10.30–16.00 Mon–Sat, 13.30–16.00 Sun.* It is also a living church and *open to the public for normal services.* Charge (unless attending service).

St Martin in the Fields   13 J 11
Trafalgar Sq WC2. 01-930 1862. Strictly speaking this is the parish church of Buckingham Palace. It is not used as such, although there is a Royal Box above the congregation, complete with fireplace. It is also the parish church of the Admiralty. It is a light and airy building, designed by James Gibbs in 1722–4, famous for its lunchtime music recitals and Christmas choral concerts. Charles II was baptised here and George I was the first churchwarden. A living church, *open to the public for normal services.*

St Paul's Cathedral   14 Z 6
Ludgate Hill EC4. 01-248 2705. Sir Christopher Wren's greatest work, built from 1675–1710 to replace a church destroyed by the Great Fire. He lies in the crypt and the Latin inscription on his tomb translates, 'Reader, if you seek a memorial look about you'. The superb dome and porches has dwarfed by modern building, but the interior has lost nothing with its magnificent stalls by Grinling Gibbons, ironwork by Tijou, paintings by Thornhill, mosaics by Salviati and Stevens. In 1981 the Prince of Wales broke with royal tradition when he married Lady Diana Spencer here instead of in Westminster Abbey which, for all its size, was deemed too small to accommodate all the illustrious guests. *Open to the public for visiting 09.00–18.00 Mon–Sat. Services only Sun. Crypt and galleries open 10.00–16.15 Mon–Fri, 11.00–16.15 Sat; closed Sun.* Free (charge for crypt and galleries).

Westminster Abbey   13 J 20
Broad Sanctuary SW1. 01-222 5152. (Properly the Collegiate Church of St Peter in Westminster.) Magnificent repository of much of the royal history of Britain, wherein God and Mammon meet on a grand scale. Begun by Edward the Confessor, near the site of an older church. Rebuilt by Henry III, who is buried before the High Altar, added to by successive kings until 1506, with the towers finished by Hawksmoor in 1734. The structure is in fine Perpendicular with a mighty and soaring Gothic nave.

The Coronation Chair, originally made for Edward I and enclosing the Stone of Scone, traditional coronation seat of the kings of Scotland, has been used for every coronation since 1308. The Abbey itself has been the setting for every coronation since 1066 (a good year, with Harold crowned in January and William the Conqueror the following Christmas).

As well as a functioning church – the visiting public are asked to respect services – this is something of a royal mausoleum. Henry VII's Chapel, or the Lady Chapel, at the far eastern end is the most beautiful in the Abbey, but the shrine of Edward the Confessor, behind the High Altar, should not be missed either. Among other royal figures entombed in this vast building are Henry III, Edward I and his wife Eleanor for whom he erected the 'Eleanor Crosses' to mark the resting places of her cortege as it made its way here. Here also lie Edward III, Richard II, Henry V in his own chapel, Edward VI, Mary I, Elizabeth I, Mary Queen of Scots, James I, Charles II, William III and George II.

Among the royal weddings that have been solemnised here are those of the present Queen, Princess Margaret, Princess Anne and most recently, in 1986, the Duke and Duchess of York. The Norman Undercroft, which contains the museum, has wax and wooden effigies of some of the buried monarchs including Edward III, Charles II and Elizabeth I, though the last is a later copy.

In addition to its royal associations, Westminster Abbey is also a rich repository of British history and culture, with a host of memorials and monuments honouring great statesmen, scientists, soldiers and luminaries of all the arts – Poet's Corner is a veritable who's who of English literature and one of the abbey's most popular attractions. *Open to the public for visiting 09.00–16.00 Mon–Fri, 09.00–14.00 & 15.45–17.00 Sat. Services only Sun.* Charge for the museum and the royal chapels.

ROYAL PARKS

London is particularly rich in parks and gardens, 10 of which are royal. These Royal Parks are still the property of the Crown and either originated as the grounds of Royal Palaces, royal residences, or as royal hunting areas.

Green Park   12 Y 16
SW1. 01-930 1793. Called Upper St James's Park when its 53 acres were enclosed and criss-crossed with walks by Charles II, Green Park is now just that – a green park. It has nice trees, a mound which

was once an ice-house and plenty of deck-chairs. It also has the Broad Walk which leads to the Victoria Memorial. Although the park was used for parades in the 18thC, and for a massive firework display to celebrate the Peace of Aix-La-Chapelle in 1748, it now has less to offer than any of the other parks – no water, no statues, no facilities, no flower beds. There are illustrious neighbours, though – Buckingham Palace to the south-west; Clarence House and St James's Palace to the east; and to the south-east the altogether prettier and more interesting St James's Park. *Open 05.00–24.00.* Free.

Greenwich Park

SE10. 01-858 2608. Traditionally the oldest of the Royal Parks (although St James's would contest this) because it was the first to be enclosed. It was fenced in 1433 by Henry V's brother the Duke of Gloucester. The park is certainly one of the most beautiful, lying beside the river and sweeping upwards into a green hill with panoramic views.

From the time of Henry VI, the Tudors had a favoured royal residence here, a palace on the site of the Duke of Gloucester's original house. It was the birthplace of Henry VIII, Edward VI, Queen Mary and Queen Elizabeth I, and reached the heights of its royal popularity in the reign of Henry VIII when jousts and tournaments were held within its boundaries. It fell from grace as a royal home in the reign of William III, whose asthma was adversely affected by the river mists, and the present elegant buildings post-date the old palace which has quite disappeared.

The three principal groups of buildings now standing are Sir Christopher Wren's magnificent Royal Naval College; the National Maritime Museum housed in two wings flanking the Queen's House, which was built by Inigo Jones for James I's Queen, Anne of Denmark; and, on the hilltop, the Old Royal Observatory, including the Great Equatorial Building, the Greenwich Meridian from which longitude is measured, and Flamsteed's House built by Wren for the first Astronomer Royal.

Just outside the park by the riverside is Sir Francis Chichester's yacht *Gipsy Moth IV* and the 19thC tea-clipper *Cutty Sark*; at the top of the park the Ranger's House, once home of the 4th Earl of Chesterfield, has a unique collection of Stuart and Jacobean paintings.

Visitors beguiled by these delights, and by the tennis courts, cricket, hockey and rugby pitches, band concerts, lake, gardens, stunning views and neat cafeteria shouldn't miss the reminders of a royal past – the small herd of deer kept in The Wilderness at the south-east corner in memory of royal hunts; the sunken bath near the Chesterfield Gate, believed to have been used in more exclusive days by Queen Caroline;

and the Queen's Oak, east of the Old Royal Observatory, a tall creeper-covered stump around which Henry VIII and Anne Boleyn are said to have danced and within which Elizabeth I is said to have picnicked. *Open 07.00–22.00 summer; 07.00–18.00 or dusk winter.* Free.

Hampton Court & Bushey Park

Middx. 01-977 1328. The two parks are divided by Hampton Court Road and have different characters despite a similar history. Both belonged to the Knights Hospitaller, both were acquired by Cardinal Wolsey and both were given to Henry VIII in an unsuccessful attempt to regain royal favour just a year or two before the Cardinal's lands were forfeit to the Crown. Bushey Park has fishing, horse riding, a boating pool, several entrances, paths and walks. Hampton Court Park (properly called Home Park) is altogether more formal and more elaborately landscaped, containing as it does that most impressive of the Royal Palaces, Hampton Court.

Bushey Park has the Royal Paddocks where royal horses are still bred and where they take their holidays, away from ceremonial duties. It also has the wondrous Chestnut Walk, planted for William III, and the Woodland Garden through which flows the Longford River, created during the reign of Charles I.

Hampton Court Park has exceptional gardens, planned in their day to rival Versailles. Their best known feature is the Maze, probably first laid out around 1670. Worthy of a longer look is the magnificent Great Fountain Garden with its ornamental yews and canals; The Long Water, created by Charles II; the herbaceous border along The Broad Walk, begun by Queen Caroline; the Old Tudor Gardens which include a formal Knot Garden and which date from Henry VIII's time; the beautiful Tijou screens which separate the gardens from the riverside; and the Great Vine which dates from 1768 and has its own personal attendant.

In common with other Royal Parks, this pair have an immense team of gardeners and a nursery for the cultivation of new plants. Both are also deer parks with herds of fallow and red deer. Although these are not hunted as they once were, they are still culled, and the resulting venison still graces royal tables. *Open 07.45–dusk.* Free. Charge for Hampton Court Palace.

Hyde Park   11 K 12

W2. 01-262 5484. The 340-acre spread was appropriated from the Abbot of Westminster by Henry VIII and he, and later Elizabeth I, hunted deer here. Cromwell sold the park off, Charles II got it back at the Restoration. It was opened to the public in the reign of James I. In 1730 Queen Caroline had the Westbourne River dammed to make the famous Serpentine, and earlier William III had lamps set along Rotten Row – originally the *route du roi* between the Palace of

Westminster and Kensington Palace – making it the first English road to be illuminated at night. Even Marble Arch, at the north east corner, has royal connections: Nash designed it as a gateway to Buckingham Palace but it was judged too narrow, moved here in 1851 as a park entrance, then left stranded when road widening in the 1900s pushed back the park's boundaries. It stands on the site of Tyburn Tree, notorious gallows, dispatcher of so many lives including that of Perkin Warbeck, pretender to the throne, executed in 1499.

Despite its allegiance to the Crown this is a park of the people, focal point of major demonstrations and of the right of free speech at Speaker's Corner where – excluding only sedition and blasphemy – any views may be voiced, including anti-royalist ones. Hyde Park is also famous as the site of the Great Exhibition of 1851, housed in Joseph Paxton's magnificent Crystal Palace, which stood between Knightsbridge and Rotten Row before its removal to South London and subsequent destruction by fire, and still holds public spectacles including immense firework displays and the 41-gun salutes fired by the Royal Artillery on certain royal occasions.

Deep within there is a wild bird sanctuary and a large nursery growing plants not only for this and other central London parks but also for Buckingham Palace and for decorative effects on State occasions.

The old tea house is now the Serpentine Gallery, with temporary art exhibitions, and the new Serpentine bars, buffet and restaurant overlook the water by the bridge, with the smaller Dell restaurant as a backup at the other end of the lake.

There are three stables around the park from which horses may be hired, and those out early will see the horses of the Household Cavalry, based at Knightsbridge Barracks, and those from the nearby Royal Mews, being exercised under the trees. *Open 05.00–24.00.* Free.

Kensington Gardens　　　**11　C　15**

W8. 01-937 4848. The 275 green acres of Kensington Gardens once belonged to the Abbey of Westminster, but Henry VIII acquired them as a royal hunting ground together with the adjoining Hyde Park. The transformation of the land into its present, elegantly civilised form began when William III bought Nottingham House to the west and commissioned Sir Christopher Wren to enlarge it into Kensington Palace. Queen Mary and later Queen Anne made their mark on the gardens, but it was George II's queen, Caroline, who enlarged them to their present size and was responsible for much of the landscaping we see today, including the Broad Walk, the Long Water and the Round Pond.

William IV opened the gardens to the public and the famous Flower Walk dates from his reign. In some ways this is the most royal of the Royal Parks, since royalty still lives in apartments in Kensington Palace, and it is always possible that one of the small children being aired by a nanny may have blue blood in its veins.

Some of the most appealing features – Peter Pan's statue, the Elfin Oak with its carvings of fairies and animals, and the Pets' Cemetery – are not royal, but the lavish Albert Memorial certainly is and so, of course, are the statues of Queen Victoria and of William III which stand outside Kensington Palace. Close to the palace don't miss the peaceful Sunken Garden (this may be admired through locked gates only, which is partly why it is so peaceful) and the sun-trap of an Orangery designed for Queen Anne. *Open 07.30–dusk.* Free. Charge for Kensington Palace.

Regent's Park　　　**4　T　11**

NW1. 01-486 7905. Once part of Henry VIII's royal hunting grounds, the park took on its present handsome form when the Prince Regent appointed John Nash to connect it by way of Regent Street to the now demolished Carlton House. The design of 1812–16 was never completed, but the 487 acres of lawns and lakes were encircled by elegant Regency terraces and imposing gateways. Here you will find the Grand Union Canal – called Regent's Canal at this point – a boating lake with 30 species of waterfowl, the exotic onion-domed mosque and, in the Inner Circle, Queen Mary's lovely Rose Gardens with its bandstand and open-air theatre where, in good weather, you can watch performances, primarily of Shakespearean plays, from May to August.

Here, too, is the famous London Zoo, containing one of the largest collections of creatures in the world. It was first laid out by Decimus Burton in 1827, with imaginative new animal houses added in recent years, on the lines of a redevelopment planned by Sir High Casson. Of these the most celebrated is probably the pointed shrugging structure that is Lord Snowdon's aviary.

Primrose Hill, a Royal Park since 1842, is under the same administration as Regent's Park but divided from it by Prince Albert Road. It is a grassy hill, suitable for kite-flying, upon which the Regent's Park nurseries hope to re-establish wild primroses, missing for many a year. *Open 05.00–dusk.* Free. *Zoo open 09.00–18.00 Mon–Sat; 10.00–19.00 Sun & Nat Hols.* Charge.

Richmond Park

Surrey. 01-940 0654. A Royal Park of 2,500 acres, first enclosed as a hunting ground by Charles I in 1637, although he preserved public rights of way and permitted people to gather fallen wood within it. It is a natural, open park of spinneys and plantations – including the quite magical Isabella Plantation – wide vistas, bracken and ancient oaks, survivors of the great oak forests of the Middle Ages. It is more like genuine countryside than any of the other Royal Parks and is rich in bird life as well as squirrels, foxes, badgers and weasels.

Its most important inhabitants are the two herds of deer, red deer and fallow deer, between 600 and 700 animals in all, which can be quite dangerous in the autumn rutting season or just after the birth of their young. They feel particularly threatened by dogs and have been known to kill them. Though they live wild they are properly managed and regular culls supply venison for the Royal Warrant list which includes the Prime Minister and the two archbishops, as well as the Royal Family.

There are two golf courses in the park; cycle tracks, plentiful car parks, fishing in Pen Ponds near the centre though you need a permit – and 12 miles of bridle ways. Those in need of refreshment should make for the Roehampton Gate, where there is a restaurant, or the Richmond Gate near which is Pembroke Lodge restaurant. The park still has royal residents – the Ogilvys live at Thatched House Lodge, between Kingston Gate and Ham Gate. The other royal building, White Lodge, is now used by the Royal Ballet School. It was built as a hunting lodge for George II and both Queen Victoria and Queen Elizabeth, the Queen Mother lived here for a while. Edward VIII was born here. It is worth noting that there are strict speed restrictions on cars passing through, heavy vehicles are not admitted, and nothing may be towed. *Open from dawn to ½-hour before dusk.* Free.

Royal Botanic Gardens

Kew, Surrey. 01-940 1171. The Royal Botanic Gardens cover 300 riverside acres. They are an important research institute, concerned with the identification, conservation and distribution of plants world-wide. The whole area is a wonderful sight, with more than 25,000 species and varieties of plants, magnificent trees, and two exceptionally fine Victorian glasshouses designed by Decimus Burton. Kew first became royal in 1731 when the then Prince of Wales took out a lease on a house which had part of the present gardens as its grounds. His widow established a small botanic garden here. George II lived at nearby Richmond Lodge which no longer exists. Later George III formally linked the two adjoining pieces of land and 'Capability' Brown developed the

Gardens, which were eventually given to the people by a Royal Commission in 1841.

Within the grounds, as well as the various plant houses, are the follies, Sir William Chamber's Orangery and Pagoda, the 225-foot-high Douglas Fir flagstaff, the cottages which house the Wood Museum, the Botanical Museum and the Marianne North collection of Botanical paintings, not to mention the two tea rooms. There are two buildings which have royal connections. One is Kew Palace, sometimes known as the Dutch House, which George III and Queen Caroline used while awaiting the building of a new summer palace that was never completed. The other is The Queen's Cottage, set in a woodland site, built as a summerhouse for Queen Charlotte and given to the nation by Queen Victoria in 1899. *Open 10.00–dusk or 20.00 summer.* Small charge.

St James's Park　　　　　**13　F　18**

SW1. 01-930 1793. Regards itself as the oldest of the Royal Parks, although it was not enclosed until 1532 whereas Greenwich Park acquired its first wooden fence in 1433. It is on the site of a 13thC hospice for leprous maidens and right in the heart of the most majestic quarter of London. The Mall, setting of much royal pageantry, is actually a part of the park.

Whether you believe Britain to be governed from Buckingham Palace, from the Houses of Parliament, from the offices and ministries along Whitehall, or even from the discreet and sober confines of the gentlemen's clubs of St James's – it all happens within a short stroll of this park. The proximity of all the government buildings ensures that politicians and civil servants are among those who enjoy the flowers, the water and the shade from the elegant trees.

The present design was achieved for George IV by John Nash in the 1820s, making this park one of the prettiest and most romantic of them all with its long lake, delicate bridge and weeping willows. The bridge, with its lovely views, was put up in 1957 replacing Nash's original.

Sporting facilities would be inappropriate here, but there is a children's playground, a bandstand with regular summertime music and a cafeteria called The Cake House at the Horse Guards Parade end. *Open 05.00–24.00.* Free.

ROYAL STREETS & WAYS

Numerous London streets are named after royal personages, and many streets are actually the property of the Crown – a major London landowner. The following, however, have even stronger royal links.

King's Road　　　　　　**19　J　13**

SW3, SW6, SW10. The section of King's Road from Sloane Square to Old Church Street once stood aloof as a private royal track used by Charles II on his way from St

James's Palace to Hampton Court Palace, and later by George III making for Kew. It remained private until 1830, but is now well-equipped with fashionable clothes and shoe shops, antique shops, restaurants and wine bars, all heavily frequented by the young and colourful.

Two other royal connections: *Rule Britannia* is thought to have been composed at No 215 by Dr Thomas Arne, and the Old Chelsea Burial Ground was made into a park-like space with plants and benches to celebrate Elizabeth II's Silver Jubilee.

The Mall   13 D 16

SW1. Wide, sweeping avenue, bordered by St James's Park, leading from Admiralty Arch to Buckingham Palace. It was laid out c1660 for Charles II and used in his time for the ball and mallet game called pall mall. Once a place where the fashionable promenaded in their best clothes, it now has moveable lamp posts and traffic islands to accommodate royal processions.

Pall Mall   13 E 14

SW1. Built to keep traffic and its concomitant dust away from the pall mall alley (The Mall – see above), which was much used for the game played by Charles II. It was originally called Catherine Street after Charles's Queen, Catherine of Braganza, but from the beginning was popularly known as Pall Mall and eventually the name stuck so fast it become official. Always fashionable, it was at one time principally residential – a daughter (Princess Christian) and two grand-daughters of Queen Victoria lived here. It is still full of fine 19thC buildings housing the private gentlemen's clubs that developed from 18thC coffee houses – the Athenaeum, the Army and Navy, the RAC, the Reform, the Travellers, the United Oxford and Cambridge and the Junior Carlton are all here.

Regent Street   13 B 10

W1. John Nash was invited by George IV, then Prince of Wales, to construct an artery from Carlton House to the royal country home near Regent's Park. He not only designed the route for Regent's Street but also most of the houses. This took many years since it was pieced together to conform with the various architectural styles along the way. Initially acclaimed, it was pulled down in 1927 (King George V and his Queen drove down its flower-decked length to celebrate the imminent destruction) and rebuilt from end to end. It is still an elegant shopping street, with the emphasis on quality merchandise, and well-endowed with royal connections. In addition to three major jewellers – Mappin and Webb, Carrington and Co, and Garrards (the Crown Jewellers) – Hamleys, Liberty and Aquascutum are also Royal Warrant holders. The Café Royal, another famous Regent Street landmark, was frequented by Edward VIII and George VI who often dined there in the years before they succeeded to the throne.

Rotten Row   11 K 17

Hyde Park W2. A wide sandy ride, where those with access to horses exercise them daily. Now more commonly known as The Mile, it was originally the *route du roi*, or King's Road, to Kensington Palace. The king who made use of it was William III, who also had it lamplit at night as a measure of protection against highwaymen and footpads – the first road in England to have this refinement.

The Silver Jubilee Walkway

The 10-mile walkway was marked out, by way of distinctive crowns set in the pavement, in 1977 in celebration of Queen Elizabeth II's Silver Jubilee. It is circular, so it is possible to begin at any point and to proceed in either direction, but the trustees suggest tackling it in seven sections: Leicester Square to Parliament Square; Parliament Square to South Bank Jubilee Gardens; South Bank Jubilee Gardens to Southwark Cathedral; Southwark Cathedral to Tower Hill Terrace; Tower Hill Terrace to St Paul's Cathedral; St Paul's Cathedral to Leicester Square; and finally the Barbican loop which takes you from St Paul's to Mansion House and passes the Museum of London.

A leaflet setting out the route and giving details of interesting points along it is available from the London Tourist Board Information Centre at Victoria Railway Station. (Note that the leaflet is 10 years old and some of its details are out of date.)

Whitehall   13 J 15

SW1. The street takes its name from the old Palace of Whitehall which once fronted on to it. The arch leading to Horse Guards Parade is still designated as a palace entrance and no-one may drive through it except the Queen, members of the immediate Royal Family, and privileged holders of an ivory pass.

The palace was a royal residence of Henry VIII (who died in it), but nowadays only the Banqueting House, a relatively late addition, remains. It continued to be a royal residence in the reigns of Edward VI, Elizabeth I, James I, Charles I and II, and James II. In the reign of William and Mary, who chose not to live here, it was accidentally burnt down.

Impressive, governmental and sometimes imperialist architecture fronts on to this wide processional way which leads towards the Houses of Parliament and ends at the Cenotaph, where the dead of two world wars are commemorated in the presence of the Queen each November.

Charles I travelled this route on the way to his trial, and was executed outside the Banqueting House.

The official residences of the Prime Minister and of the Chancellor of the Exchequer are in Downing Street, just off Whitehall – the heartland of the administration of Great Britain.

SHOPS & SERVICES BY ROYAL APPOINTMENT

Royal Warrants of Appointment to Her Majesty Queen Elizabeth II relate to four separate departments – the Department of Her Majesty's Privy Purse, the Department of the Master of the Household, the Lord Chamberlain's Office, and the Royal Mews Department. The three other members of the Royal Family to grant Royal Warrants are Queen Elizabeth, the Queen Mother, His Royal Highness the Duke of Edinburgh, and His Royal Highness the Prince of Wales.

Warrant holders are entitled to display the relevant Royal Arms, but not to fly the Royal Standard. They are entitled to style themselves 'By Appointment to . . .', but should not use the word royal, as in 'By Royal Appointment', without first checking with the Secretary of the Royal Household Tradesmen's Warrants Committee.

Warrants are awarded to manufacturers, wholesalers and retailers throughout Britain and overseas. The list below includes retailers within London only, but omits suppliers of such appealing items as bagpipes, tartans, dog and game food (Scotland); champagne (France); honey (Orkney); organ blower manufacturers (Wareham) and numerous others. Anyone caring to see the full list should buy the relevant *Supplement to The London Gazette*, which comes out early in January and is available from HMSO.

Occasionally a shop or store with a wide range of stock holds a warrant for one specific type of merchandise only; where this is the case it has been indicated in the text.

Opening Times

Most shops are *open between 09.00/09.30 and 17.30 Mon–Sat* and are *closed on Sun and Nat Hols.* West End shops stay *open late on Thur to 19.30/20.00*; Knightsbridge, Sloane Square and King's Road shops stay *open on Wed to 19.30/20.00.* Some Bond Street shops are *closed all day Sat.* Where a shop's opening times differ from the standards above, the difference is noted in italics at the end of the entry.

Accessories

Eximious   **20 S   1**
10 West Halkin St SW1. 01-627 2888. Monogrammed accessories, especially luggage, leather wallets and jewel cases. By appointment to the Prince of Wales. *Closes 13.00 Sat.*

Antiques & Objets d'Art

Halcyon Days   **12 Y   8**
105 New Bond St W1. 01-629 8811. Charm-

ing collection of objets d'art, including enamels designed and made solely for the shop. By appointment to the Queen and the Queen Mother. *Closes 16.30 Sat.*

S. J. Phillips   **12 Y   8**
139 New Bond St W1. 01-629 6261. General antique dealers with a good stock of continental silver and snuff boxes. Their first Royal Appointment was to the late Queen Mary. Now by appointment to the Queen Mother. *Open 10.00–17.00 Mon–Sat.*

Bakers

Justin de Blank   **20 O   2**
46 Walton St SW3. 01-589 4734. Bakery producing fine wholesome bread. There are also retail delicatessens selling high-quality groceries at 42 Elizabeth St SW1; 54 Duke St W1; 115 Randall Rd SE11; 60 New King's Rd SW3; and a herb and flower shop at 114 Ebury St SW1. Bakery by appointment to the Queen.

Books

J. A. Allen   **20 Y   1**
1 Lower Grosvenor Pl SW1. 01-828 8855/834 5606. Publishers and suppliers of equine and equestrian literature. By appointment to the Queen and the Duke of Edinburgh. *Closes 13.00 Sat.*

Hatchards   **13 C 12**
187 Piccadilly W1. 01-439 9921. Reliable and knowledgeable general booksellers, established in 1797. By appointment to the Queen, the Queen Mother, the Duke of Edinburgh and the Prince of Wales. *Closes 13.00 Sat.*

Maggs Bros   **12 Y 11**
50 Berkeley Sq W1. 01-493 7160. Purveyors of rare books and manuscripts. By appointment to the Queen. *Closed Sat.*

A. R. Mowbrays   **13 A   4**
28 Margaret St W1. 01-580 8614. Theological and general booksellers and suppliers of fine bindings. By appointment to the Queen Mother. *Closed Sat.*

Boots

John Lobb   **13 B 14**
9 St James's St SW1. 01-930 3664. Family firm of bootmakers, established more than 130 years ago, who have supplied the Royal Family since 1911. By appointment to the Queen, the Duke of Edinburgh and the Prince of Wales. *Closes 13.00 Sat.*

Henry Maxwell   **13 A 10**
11 Savile Row W1. 01-734 9714. Bespoke boot and shoemaker with only a small stock

of ready-to-wear shoes for men. By appointment to the Queen. *Closes 13.00–14.00 daily & Sat.*

Brushes

Temple & Crook   **12 S 20**
3 Kinnerton St SW1. 01-235 2166. In an attractive street in smart Belgravia – a supplier of brushes and hardware. By appointment to the Queen. *Closes 13.00 Sat.*

Butchers

J. H. Dewhurst   **14 Y 1**
Head Office, 14 West Smithfield EC1. 01-248 1212. Supplies its own chain of high street butchers' shops, with branches throughout London and the suburbs. By appointment to the Queen.
John Lidstone   **20 W 3**
12 Lower Belgrave St SW1. 01-730 9373. Suppliers of Scotch beef, English lamb and other meats. By appointment to the Queen and the Queen Mother. *Closes 13.00 Sat.*

Car Hire

Godfrey Davis Europcar   **20 Z 4**
Davis House, Wilton Rd SW1. 01-834 8484. The head office of a firm which has numerous branches, including ones at all main-line railway stations and London Heathrow airport. By appointment to the Queen.

Cheese

Paxton & Whitfield   **13 B 13**
93 Jermyn St SW1. 01-930 9892. Provision merchants founded (though not on this site) in 1740, with a hugely impressive range of cheeses in perfect condition. By appointment to the Queen Mother.

Chemists

Ainsworth's   **12 X 1**
38 New Cavendish St W1. 01-935 5330. Homeopathic pharmacy. By appointment to the Queen and the Queen Mother.
D. R. Harris   **13 B 13**
29 St James's St SW1. 01-930 3915. Conventional pharmacy, established in 1790. By appointment to the Queen Mother.

China & Glass

Thomas Goode   **12 V 12**
19 South Audley St W1. 01-499 2823. Gleaming, glittering displays of beautiful china and glass. By appointment to the Queen, the Queen Mother and the Prince of Wales.

Chocolates

Charbonnel et Walker   **13 A 12**
28 Old Bond St W1. 01-629 4396. Founded by Mlle Charbonnel in 1874. Hand-made, usually soft-centred chocolates, arranged in beautiful presentation boxes. By appointment to the Queen.
Prestat   **12 W 7**
40 South Molton St W1. 01-629 4838. Purveyors of fine chocolates – all hand-made on the premises. Fresh cream truffles a speciality. By appointment to the Queen.

Coffee

H. R. Higgins (Coffee Man)   **12 V 7**
79 Duke St W1. 01-629 3913. Over 40 different types of coffee, original and blended, light and dark roast. By appointment to the Queen.
Savoy Hotel Coffee Dept   **13 M 10**
Savoy Hotel WC2. 01-836 4343. Bulk orders go through the Coffee Department, but those wanting the odd half-pound should call at the foyer gift shop. By appointment to the Queen. *Open 07.00–22.00 Mon–Sun.*

Coins & Medals

B. A. Seaby   **12 Y 4**
8 Cavendish Sq W1. 01-631 3707. One of the largest coin shops in the world, with eight experts. By appointment to the Queen.
Spink & Son   **13 C 14**
5 King St SW1. 01-930 7888. Stockists of coins and can acquire any coin wanted by a collector. They are also medallists, by appointment to the Queen, the Duke of Edinburgh and the Prince of Wales.

Dressmakers

Hardy Amies   **13 A 10**
14 Savile Row W1. 01-734 2436. Internationally famous couturier – by appointment to the Queen. *Essential to make an appointment.*
Norman Hartnell   **12 Y 10**
26 Bruton St W1. 01-629 0992. The business was launched in 1924 by the first London-based designer to hold a dress show in Paris. By appointment to the Queen and the Queen Mother. *Essential to make an appointment.*

Ecclesiastical Furnishings

Watts & Co   **21 H 2**
7 Tufton St SW1. 01-222 7169. Complete church furnishers appropriately sited just along the road from The United Society for the Propagation of the Gospel. By appointment to the Queen. *Appointment advisable.*

Embroidery & Insignia

S. Lock   **13 E 3**
34 Rathbone Pl W1. 01-636 0574. Bespoke

couture and stage embroidery and beading – tailored to customers' requirements. By appointment to the Queen. *Essential to make an appointment.*

Toye, Kenning & Spencer   13 M 5
19 Great Queen St WC2. 01-242 0471. Suppliers of gold and silver laces, insignia and embroidery. (Also supply masonic regalia, but not by appointment.) By appointment to the Queen. *Essential to make an appointment.*

Fancy Goods

Forces Help Society &   19 M 1
Lord Roberts Workshops
122 Brompton Rd SW3. 01-589 3243. Brushware and furniture made in their own workshops by disabled ex-servicemen. Manufacturers of fancy goods by appointment to the Queen. Furniture makers by appointment to the Queen Mother. *Closed Sat.*

General Trading Company   20 R 6
144 Sloane St SW1. 01-730 0411. China, glass, small items of furniture and upmarket gifts at the well-known repository of royal wedding lists. Suppliers of fancy goods by appointment to the Queen, the Queen Mother, the Duke of Edinburgh and the Prince of Wales.

Fish

W. F. Sproston   22 R 16
17 Claylands Pl SW8. 01-735 3331. Principally wholesalers of fresh and frozen fish, who smoke their own salmon on the premises. Open to the public a few mornings a week. By appointment to the Queen, the Queen Mother and the Prince of Wales. *Open 09.30–12.00 Tue–Fri only.*

Fishing Tackle

C. Farlow   13 E 14
5 Pall Mall SW1. 01-839 2423. Specialists in game fishing tackle and suitably waterproof clothing, established in 1840. All the staff are anglers. By appointment to the Prince of Wales.

Flags

Black & Edgington Hire   16 O 17
29 Queen Elizabeth St SE1. 01-407 3734. Hirers of flags and tentage who also have a manufacturing division making flags of all nations and for numerous companies. Flagmakers by appointment to the Queen. *Closes 16.30 Mon–Fri & all day Sat.*

Flowers

Edward Goodyear   11 L 18
43 Knightsbridge SW1. 01-235 8344. Fragrant florists with two retail outlets and a delivery service. Also at 45 Bruton St W1.

By appointment to the Queen, the Queen Mother, the Duke of Edinburgh and the Prince of Wales.

Moyses Stevens   12 Y 10
6 Bruton St W1. 01-493 8171. Fresh and dried flowers delivered throughout London. By appointment to the Queen Mother.

Forage

Anstee & Co
187 Wandsworth High St SW18. 01-874 4193. Corn and hay merchants, with a cash and carry service for forage. They supply fodder to the Metropolitan Police horses as well as to the Royal Mews. By appointment to the Queen.

Furs

Calman Links   12 O 20
241 Brompton Rd SW1. 01-581 1927. Top-quality fur coats and jackets. By appointment to the Queen and the Queen Mother.

Guns

Holland & Holland   12 Y 10
33 Bruton St W1. 01-499 4411. Top London gunsmiths and rifle makers. By appointment to the Duke of Edinburgh. *Closed Sat.*

James Purdey & Sons   12 V 12
57 South Audley St W1. 01-499 5292. Established in 1814 as gunmakers and cartridge makers, with a portrait gallery of distinguished past patrons. By appointment to the Queen, the Duke of Edinburgh and the Prince of Wales. *Closed Sat.*

John Rigby   13 K 9
5 King St WC2. 01-734 7611. Manufacturers of, and dealers in, high-quality, handmade, modern sporting guns and rifles. By appointment to the Queen. *Closed Sat.*

Hairdressers

Maurice and Robert   19 H 4
8 Thurloe Pl SW7. 01-584 4433. Court hairdressers. By appointment to the Queen Mother.

Geo. F. Trumper   12 W 13
9 Curzon St W1. 01-499 1850. Hairdresser and perfumier with real sponges and badger bristle shaving brushes in the window. By appointment to the Queen.

Hats

Frederick Fox   12 Y 9
87 New Bond St W1. 01-629 5706. Milliners creating model hats. By appointment to the Queen.

Herbert Johnson   13 A 10
13 Old Burlington St W1. 01-439 7397. Hats for men and women for all occasions. By appointment to the Queen and the Prince of Wales.

James Lock   **13**   **B**   **14**
6 St James's St SW1. 01-930 8874. Gentlemen's hatters who have been established here since 1765. By appointment to the Duke of Edinburgh.

Simone Mirman   **20**   **S**   **1**
11a West Halkin St SW1. 01-235 2656. Unusual high-fashion hats and accessories. By appointment to the Queen and the Queen Mother.

Jewellers, Goldsmiths & Silversmiths

Asprey's   **12**   **Y**   **8**
165 New Bond St W1. 01-493 6767. Antique and modern jewellery, the work of goldsmiths and silversmiths, luxury luggage and gifts. By appointment to the Queen, the Queen Mother and the Prince of Wales. *Closes 13.00 Sat.*

Carrington & Co   **13**   **B**   **10**
170 Regent St W1. 01-734 3727. Silversmiths and jewellers – makers of the crown worn by Queen Alexandra at the coronation of Edward VII. By appointment to the Queen and the Queen Mother.

Cartier   **12**   **Y**   **8**
175 New Bond St W1. 01-493 6962. Top-class internationally-famous jewellers and goldsmiths. By appointment to the Queen and the Queen Mother.

Collingwood of Bond Street   **12**   **Y**   **8**
171 New Bond St W1. 01-499 5613. Long-established royal jewellers selling antique and modern gold and silverware. By appointment to the Queen, the Queen Mother and the Prince of Wales.

Garrard & Co   **13**   **C**   **10**
112 Regent St W1. 01-734 7020. Fine jewellery, antique and modern silver and gold, from the Crown Jewellers. By appointment to the Queen and the Queen Mother.

Paul Longmire   **13**   **C**   **13**
12 Bury St SW1. 01-930 8720. Jewellers and silversmiths in a street owned by The Crown. Jewellery and leather goods by appointment to the Queen. Silver and presentation gifts by appointment to the Queen Mother.

Mappin & Webb   **13**   **C**   **10**
170 Regent St W1. 01-439 8297. High-quality modern jewellery and silver with branches at 65 Brompton Rd SW3, 2 Queen Victoria St EC4 and 125 Fenchurch St EC3. By appointment to the Queen and the Prince of Wales.

Wartski   **12**   **Z**   **10**
14 Grafton St W1. 01-493 1141. Classy jewellers. By appointment to the Queen, the Queen Mother and the Prince of Wales.

Laundry & Dry Cleaning

Lilliman & Cox   **12**   **Y**   **9**
34 Bruton Pl W1. 01-491 1644. Dry cleaners, specialising in beaded and embroidered dresses. By appointment to the Queen, the Queen Mother and the Prince of Wales.

Sycamore Laundry and Dry Cleaners
4 Old Town SW4. 01-622 3333. Launderers and dry cleaners. By appointment to the Queen, the Queen Mother, the Duke of Edinburgh and the Prince of Wales.

Linen

Vantona International   **12**   **Y**   **7**
Linen Company
20 Brook St W1. 01-629 5000. Table linen and monogrammed handkerchiefs, sold in a rather grand atmosphere. By appointment to the Queen.

Luggage

Mayfair Trunks   **12**   **X**   **14**
3 Shepherd St W1. 01-499 2620. Suppliers of all types and sizes of cases and trunks. By appointment to the Queen and the Queen Mother.

Mackintoshes

Aquascutum   **13**   **C**   **10**
100 Regent St W1. 01-734 6090. Coats, suits, knitwear, accessories, but principally known as makers of weatherproof garments. By appointment to the Queen Mother.

Burberrys   **13**   **C**   **10**
161 Regent St W1. 01-734 4060. Co-ordinated hats, scarves, accessories and distinctive, classic raincoats for men and women. Knitwear, suits, smart casual fashions as well. Also have a branch at 18 Haymarket SW1. By appointment to the Queen and the Queen Mother.

Motor Body Builders

James Asbridge
60 Banning St, Greenwich SW10. 01-858 0057. Repairer and painter of horsedrawn vehicles. By appointment to the Queen. *Essential to make an appointment.*

Newsagents

Jones Yarrell   **15**   **K**   **15**
227 Tooley St SE1. 01-407 6267. Newsagents who deliver. By appointment to the Queen, the Queen Mother, the Duke of Edinburgh and the Prince of Wales.

Opticians

Theodore Hamblin   **12**   **W**   **4**
7 Wigmore St W1. 01-935 3615. Sharing the street with the world-famous Wigmore Hall is this optician with branches in several London high streets. By appointment to the

Queen, the Queen Mother and the Duke of Edinburgh.

Perfumiers

J. Floris **13 B 13**
89 Jermyn St SW1. 01-930 2885. Perfumiers to the Court of St James since George IV, specialising in English flower perfumes and preparations for men. By appointment to the Queen and the Prince of Wales.

Penhaligon's **13 M 8**
41 Wellington St WC2. 01-836 2150. Traditional toiletries, hand-made fragrances, old English silver scent bottles. By appointment to the Duke of Edinburgh.

Photographic Equipment

Wallace Heaton **12 X 7**
127 New Bond St W1. 01-629 7511. High-quality photographic, cine and projection equipment. By appointment to the Queen, the Queen Mother, the Duke of Edinburgh and the Prince of Wales.

Pianos

Steinway & Sons **12 V 5**
Steinway Hall, 44 Marylebone Lane W1. 01-487 3391. Manufacturers and purveyors of pianos since 1853. By appointment to the Queen.

Picture Frames

Arnold Wiggins & Sons **2 S 19**
30 Woodfield Pl W9. 01-286 9656. Antique picture frames. By appointment to the Queen and the Queen Mother. *Essential to make an appointment.*

Robes

Ede & Ravenscroft **14 R 4**
93 Chancery Lane WC2. 01-405 3906. Makers of ceremonial, academic and legal robes. Chancery Lane is where heralds traditionally announce the accession to the throne of the sovereign. By appointment to the Queen, the Queen Mother, the Duke of Edinburgh and the Prince of Wales. *Closed Sat.*

Saddles

W. & H. Gidden **13 A 9**
15d Clifford St W1. 01-734 2788. Reliable saddlers in an elegant 18thC street. By appointment to the Queen.

Shirts

Ashley & Blake **19 M 1**
42 Beauchamp Pl SW3. 01-584 2682. Classic ready-made gentlemen's shirts in good

fabrics. By appointment to the Duke of Edinburgh.

Thresher & Glenny **14 N 9**
Lancaster Pl WC2. 01-836 4608. The oldest private trader to hold a Royal Warrant. They produce their own design of classical, plain and striped shirts in best cotton. Also at 50 Gresham St EC2. By appointment to the Queen and the Queen Mother. *Closed Sat.*

Turnbull & Asser **13 B 12**
71 Jermyn St W1. 01-930 0502. Ready-made and bespoke English cottons and silks. Also at 23 Bury St SW1. By appointment to the Prince of Wales.

Shoes & Bags

H. & M. Rayne **12 O 19**
57 Brompton Rd SW3. 01-589 5560. Smart shoes and handbags. Many branches. By appointment to the Queen and the Queen Mother.

Stamps

Stanley Gibbons **13 L 10**
399 Strand WC2. 01-836 8444. World-famous philatelists stocking everything from new issues to classics. Excellent catalogues. By appointment to the Queen.

Stationery

Frank Smythson **12 Y 7**
54 New Bond St W1. 01-629 8558. Quality stationery, die-stamping, copper plate invitations and visiting cards, leather desk-top equipment, leather-bound diaries and address books. By appointment to the Queen. *Closes 12.30 Sat & all day Sat preceding Nat Hols.*

Stores

Army & Navy Stores **21 D 3**
105 Victoria St SW1. 01-834 1234. Excellent food hall and wine department, clothes, cosmetics, toys, books, china and glass, hairdressing salon, coffee shop and restaurant. Household and fancy goods by appointment to the Queen and the Queen Mother.

Fortnum & Mason **13 C 12**
181 Piccadilly W1. 01-734 8040. Decorous department store of international renown, particularly for its food hall full of bottled and canned exotica, delicatessen delicacies, top-quality meats and cheeses, and superb hampers. The floor-walkers in bright red morning dress provide assistance with yesteryear courtesy. Also sells luxury goods and designer collection clothes. Grocers and provision merchants by appointment to the Queen; leather and fancy goods by appointment to the Queen Mother.

Harrods **12 N 20**
Knightsbridge SW1. 01-730 1234. The

world's most famous department store, which prides itself on selling virtually everything. Fashions and accessories, perfumery, gifts, china and glass, pets, toys, books, furniture, fabrics, pictures, pianos. Magnificent, Edwardian marble food halls, hairdressers and barbers, restaurants, tea and coffee shops and a wide range of services. Its January sale is one of the capital's top shopping events. Suppliers of provisions and household goods by appointment to the Queen and the Queen Mother; outfitters by appointment to the Duke of Edinburgh; outfitters and saddlers by appointment to the Prince of Wales.

Heal & Son   **5   D   20**
196 Tottenham Court Rd W1. 01-636 1666. Huge selection of the best of contemporary British and continental furniture and a large range of modern fabrics in every type of weave and design. Upholsterers and suppliers of bedding by appointment to the Queen.

Harvey Nichols   **12   P   18**
Knightsbridge SW1. 01-235 5000. Clothes and accessories from top British, continental and American designers, stylish fabrics, home furnishings and household goods. Drapers by appointment to the Queen Mother; purveyors of household and fancy goods by appointment to the Prince of Wales.

Peter Jones   **20   P   7**
Sloane Sq SW1. 01-730 3434. Modern and antique furniture, furnishing fabrics and linens, household goods, glass, china, fashions, hairdressing and even interpreters. Draper and furnisher by appointment to the Queen Mother.

Liberty   **13   A   7**
210–220 Regent St W1. 01-734 1234. Landmark store with half-timbered façade and Tudor-style interior. Fashionable and famous, especially for its distinctive printed fabrics. Also sells designer clothes, oriental rugs, pictures and gifts, glass, china and costume jewellery. Silk mercers by appointment to the Queen Mother.

Lillywhites   **13   E   11**
Piccadilly Circus W1. 01-930 3181. Top English and continental equipment and clothes for most sports; a pro is available for each sport to advise on purchases. Outfitters by appointment to the Queen.

Simpson   **13   D   11**
203 Piccadilly W1. 01-734 2002. High-quality clothing for men and women. Suits, dresses, separates, country clothes and sportswear, luggage and accessories. Also a restaurant, wine bar and barber's shop. Outfitters by appointment to the Queen, the Duke of Edinburgh and the Prince of Wales.

Tailors & Outfitters

Billings & Edmonds   **12   X   6**
24 Dering St W1. 01-499 5754. Bespoke tailor and supplier of ready-made men's clothes. Tailors and outfitters by appointment to the Queen.

Burtons   **13   B   10**
114 Regent St W1. 01-734 1951. Men's clothes – suits, casual wear and accessories at reasonable prices. Many branches. By appointment to the Queen Mother.

J. Dege & Sons   **13   A   9**
16 Clifford St W1. 01-734 2248. Civilian and military tailors in one of the street's original 18thC houses. By appointment to the Queen.

Gieves & Hawkes   **13   A   10**
1 Savile Row W1. 01-434 2001. Classic but fashionable bespoke and ready-made clothes. By appointment to the Prince of Wales.

Hawes & Curtis   **13   A   11**
2 Burlington Gdns W1. 01-493 2200. Tailors and shirtmakers, founded in 1913. By appointment to the Duke of Edinburgh.

Horne Brothers   **13   L   10**
125 Strand WC2. 01-836 8351. Livery tailors by appointment to the Queen. *Essential to make an appointment.*

Johns & Pegg   **13   A   9**
4 Clifford St W1. 01-734 1713. Military tailors in premises within one of the original 18thC houses. By appointment to the Duke of Edinburgh and the Prince of Wales.

Meyer & Mortimer   **13   B   11**
6 Sackville St W1. 01-734 3135. Military outfitters by appointment to the Queen.

Henry Poole & Co   **13   A   10**
15 Savile Row W1. 01-734 5985. Livery outfitters. By appointment to the Queen.

Bernard Weatherill   **13   A   10**
8 Savile Row W1. 01-734 6905. Sporting tailors; riding clothes outfitters and livery tailors by appointment to the Queen, the Queen Mother and the Duke of Edinburgh.

Tea

R. Twining   **13   L   10**
216 Strand WC2. 01-353 3511. The trade sign above the door, of two Chinese figures, is a reminder that Indian teas were not readily available here until 1832. Tea and coffee merchants by appointment to the Queen and the Queen Mother.

Toys

Hamleys   **13   A   8**
188 Regent St W1. 01-734 3161. London's largest toy shop, its six floors richly stocked with delights for all ages. Toy and sports merchants by appointment to the Queen.

Undergarments

Rigby & Peller   **12   W   7**
12 South Molton St W1. 01-629 6708. Old-established corsetieres. By appointment to the Queen.

Whips & Gloves

Swaine, Adeney, Briggs & Sons *13 C 12*
185 Piccadilly W1. 01-734 4277. World-famous for hand-made Brigg umbrellas and luxury goods. Whip and glove manufacturers by appointment to the Queen; umbrella makers by appointment to the Queen Mother.

Window Cleaners

Mayfair Window Cleaning Company
374 Wandsworth Rd SW8. 01-720 6447. Window cleaning contractors. By appointment to the Queen Mother.

Wine & Spirit Merchants

Berry Bros & Rudd *13 B 13*
3 St James's St SW1. 01-930 1888. Charming, old, independent wine merchant's shop with first-class list. By appointment to the Queen.

Christopher & Co *13 C 12*
4 Ormond Yard SW1. 01-930 5557. Good, sound, old-fashioned wine merchants. By appointment to the Queen.

Corney & Barrow *15 F 2*
118 Moorgate EC2. 01-638 3124. Wine merchants, with branches in Helmet Row EC1 and 44 Cannon St EC4. They have a stylish, modern restaurant at the Moorgate address (for reservations telephone 01-628 2898), with an English and French menu strong on fish and game. By appointment to the Queen and the Prince of Wales.

John Harvey & Sons *13 E 14*
27 Pall Mall SW1. 01-839 4691. Long-established group with an excellent list of wines. By appointment to the Queen.

Justerini & Brooks *13 B 13*
61 St James's St SW1. 01-493 8721. Originally established in Pall Mall in 1749. By appointment to the Queen.

Saccone & Speed *13 C 9*
21 Golden Sq W1. 01-734 2061. A chain with many branches. By appointment to the Queen.

H. Allen Smith *13 D 1*
24 Scala St W1. 01-637 0387. Wine coopers and merchants, with other branches. By appointment to the Queen Mother.

FAMILY BUSINESSES

The family business may simply be 'being a Royal', but there are also some extremely well-connected people who run commercial businesses. So if you are seeking portrait photography, are keen to throw a good party, or want to buy furniture designed especially for your house, you could encounter one of them.

Patrick Lichfield *10 R 15*
(Professional Photographer)
20 Aubrey Walk W8. 01-727 4468. Patrick Lichfield is also the 5th Earl of Lichfield, a cousin to the Queen, with a family seat at Shugborough Hall, Stafford. His publications include: *The Most Beautiful Women* and *Lichfield On Photography*, 1981; *A Royal Album* and *Patrick Lichfield's Unipart Calendar Book*, 1982; *Patrick Lichfield Creating The Unipart Calendar*, 1983.

David Linley's
1 New King's Rd SW3. 01-736 6886. David Linley is also Viscount Linley, son of Princess Margaret and Lord Snowdon, and 10th in line of succession to the throne. In partnership with Matthew Rice he designs office and domestic furniture in fine woods with marquetry decoration. Almost everything is made to commission, although the showroom does carry some stock and also a range of elegant desk-top furniture. Viscount Linley is based at the showroom but is frequently away supervising one of the teams of skilled craftsmen. *Open 10.00–18.00 Mon–Fri; 11.00–17.00 Sat.*

Party Planners *10 N 8*
56 Ladbroke Grove W11. 01-229 9666. Run by Lady Elizabeth Anson, a cousin of the Queen, Party Planners offers ideas, advice, staff, cutlery, china and glass, food, wine, flowers, music and any other possible requirement for any type of party. Cocktail parties, dances, weddings, children's parties, director's lunches, conferences, dinner parties – indeed all parties – are planned and organised down to the last detail. *Open for reservations 09.30–17.30 Mon–Fri.*

Lord Snowdon *19 A 2*
(Professional Photographer & Designer)
22 Launceston Pl W8. Married to Princess Margaret (the Queen's sister) until 1978, the first Earl of Snowdon was a professional photographer, as Antony Armstrong-Jones, before the title was bestowed. He has been artistic adviser to the *Sunday Times* and Sunday Times Publications since 1962, and has had numerous exhibitions. He also designed the aviary at London Zoo, has made several TV films including the award-winning *Don't Count The Candles* in 1968 and his publications include *London* and *Malta* (the latter in collaboration), 1958; *Private View* (in collaboration) 1965; *A View of Venice* and *Assignments*, 1972; *Pride Of The Shires* and *Personal View*, 1979; *Sittings*, 1983.

MUSEUMS & GALLERIES

London's museums and art galleries are among the richest in the world. A large proportion of the material they own is not generally on view – some tends to be stored away for lack of display space – though access to it is usually possible for anyone with a genuine interest. The following is merely a selection concentrating on those which display a significant amount of material with royal connections.

Bankside Gallery   **15 A 11**
48 Hopton St SE1. 01-928 7521. Attractive gallery on the refurbished waterfront which mounts prestige exhibitions and retrospectives. It is the home of the Royal Society of Painters in Watercolours and the Royal Society of Painter-Etchers and Engravers, who exhibit twice a year; the former was founded in 1804, the latter in 1880. There is sometimes a charge and the pictures are sometimes for sale. *Open 10.00–17.00 Tue–Sat; 14.00–18.00 Sun. Closed Mon, Nat Hols & between exhibitions.*

British Museum   **13 H 1**
Great Russell St WC1. 01-636 1555. The King's Gallery is the oldest part of the present building which was designed by Sir Robert Smirke and which went up between 1823 and 1847. It contains a Royal Library of books owned by British sovereigns from Henry VIII to Charles II, which was presented by George II in 1757; and also 120,800 books from George III's library which were acquired in 1823. Displays in the King's Gallery change but *Magna Carta* is always on show.

This is one of the greatest and most richly stocked museums anywhere, with exhibits from most countries of the world and most periods of history. Among the most famous are the so-called Elgin Marbles, the Egyptian Mummies, the Rosetta Stone and the Sutton Hoo Ship Burial of an early Saxon King. The circular, domed reading room, 1857, by Sidney Smirke, in which the contents of the British Library may be studied, is for those with reader's tickets only. *Open 10.00–17.00 Mon–Sat; 14.30–18.00 Sun. Free.*

Household Cavalry Museum
Combermere Barracks, St Leonard's Rd, Windsor, Berks. (0753) 868222 ext 203. The Household Cavalry, made up of the Life Guards and the Blues and Royals, is the Sovereign's personal bodyguard, who also have a base at Hyde Park Barracks in Knightsbridge and who mount guard at Horse Guards. This, their regimental museum, contains uniforms, weapons, lavishly embroidered saddle cloths and other related items, some of them presented to the museum by the Royal Family. *Open 10.00–13.00 & 14.00–17.00 Mon–Fri; 14.00–*

17.00 Sun between 10th May & 7th Sep only. Closed Sat & Nat Hols. Free.

Madame Tussaud's   **4 S 18**
Marylebone Rd NW1. 01-935 6861. This world-famous exhibition of startlingly lifelike wax effigies of the famous and notorious (dressed wherever possible in the subject's own clothes) includes a Grand Hall in which royal families, past and present, British and foreign, are grouped most effectively near unusually silent politicians and world leaders. *Open 10.00–18.00 Mon–Sun; closes 17.50 winter.* Charge. Special Ticket includes admission to the Planetarium next door.

Museum of London   **15 B 2**
London Wall EC2. 01-600 3699. The story of the capital from prehistory to the present day is laid out in an ultra-modern setting, and inevitably includes royal material, especially in the section entitled Ceremonial London where mementoes of lavish royal and state occasions may be encountered – the present Queen's Coronation Glove, Queen Victoria's crown (minus jewels) and souvenirs of coronation mugs among them. *Open 10.00–18.00 Tue–Sat; 14.00–18.00 Sun. Closed Mon & winter Nat Hols. Free.*

National Gallery   **13 H 11**
Trafalgar Sq WC2. 01-839 3321. One of the finest collections of paintings in the world, including the national collection of European Old Masters. Here are magnificent works by Leonardo da Vinci Raphael, Botticelli, Titian, Rembrandt, Rubens, Van Dyck, El Greco, Constable, Turner, Gainsborough and Reynolds. Several are of royal interest, among them the *Wilton Diptych* in which Richard II is presented to the Virgin and child, surrounded by angels wearing his White Hart badge; an idealised equestrian Charles I by Van Dyck; and Lawrence's arresting *Queen Charlotte*. *Open 10.00–18.00 Mon–Sat; 14.00–18.00 Sun. Closed some Nat Hols. Free.*

National Maritime Museum
Romney Rd, Greenwich SE10. 01-858 4422. This is the world's largest museum on its subject, whose purpose is the study and display of material on all imaginable aspects of British maritime history. The museum is located in two wings flanking the Queen's House, which was designed by Inigo Jones for James I's Queen, Anne of Denmark, and has recently been refurbished into a small stately home of the period. Among the huge array of fascinating exhibits in the wings is the 18thC golden Royal Barge of Prince Frederick, in its own Barge House. Here too are the stories of the Royal Navy and the Royal Dockyards and, high on the hill behind, the old Royal Observatory buildings (The Observatory itself is now based at Herstmonceaux in

Sussex), and the Wren house built for the first Astronomer Royal. *Open 10.00–18.00 Mon–Sat in summer; 10.00–17.00 Mon–Sat in winter; 14.00–17.00 Sun.* Charge.

National Portrait Gallery   13 H 11
2 St Martin's Pl WC2. 01-930 1552. Important repository of contemporary portraits of major figures in British history, among them pictures or effigies of every British monarch since William the Conqueror. Don't miss the magnificent *Elizabeth I* by Marcus Gheeraerts the Younger, known as the 'Ditchley Portrait'; the Hans Holbein drawing of Henry VIII, or the collection of modern portraits of the present Royal Family, including Brian Organ's somewhat controversial paintings of the Prince and Princess of Wales. *Open 10.00–17.00 Mon–Fri; 10.00–18.00 Sat; 14.00–18.00 Sun. Closed Nat Hols.* Free (occasional charge for special exhibitions).

National Postal Museum   14 Z 4
King Edward St EC1. 01-432 3851. Behind the statue of Sir Rowland Hill, originator of the Penny Post, stands a large Post Office within which you will encounter one of the largest and most significant stamp collections in the world. Here are the stamp archives of the Royal Mint and also examples of all stamps issued by the Post Office since 1840, including celebration issues for royal events. *Open 10.00–16.30 Mon–Thur; 10.00–16.00 Fri. Closed weekends & Nat Hols.* Free.

Prince Henry's Room   14 R 7
17 Fleet St EC4. 01-353 7323. Erected in 1610 as a tavern called The Prince's Arms and now used for a small exhibition on Samuel Pepys. It is now thought to be a myth that the famous first-floor room was designed for Prince Henry, elder brother of Charles I, since the name's name was on record before he was born. Nevertheless the fine Jacobean ceiling is decorated with the three feathers of the Prince of Wales and the initials PH. *Open 13.45–17.00 Mon–Fri; 13.45–16.30 Sat. Closed mornings & Sun.* Small charge.

Queen's Gallery   12 Z 19
Buckingham Palace, Buckingham Palace Rd SW1. 01-930 4832 ext 351. The one-room gallery, formerly a private chapel, is reached through its own side entrance – you don't get to go into the palace itself. Here the priceless paintings, drawings, china and furniture of the Royal Collection are presented in small, changing exhibitions, planned so that most of the works of art in this vast and important collection are made available to the public gaze at some time or another. *Open 11.00–17.00 Tue–Sat; 14.00–17.00 Sun. Closed Mon.* Charge.

Royal Academy of Arts   13 B 11
Burlington House, Piccadilly W1. 01-734 9052. The sculpture in the entrance quadrangle is of the founder, Sir Joshua Reynolds, and the Instrument of Foundation was signed by its first royal patron,

George III. A series of important special-loan exhibitions are held here throughout the year, always containing work by major artists, and often putting before the public pictures held in private collections. During the Summer Exhibition from May to August the work of living artists is displayed. Burlington House is also the HQ of the Society of Antiquaries, the Geological Society, the Royal Society of Chemistry, the Royal Astronomical Society and the Linnean Society, but these rooms are private. *Open 10.00–18.00 Mon–Sun.* Charge.

Royal Mews   20 Y 1
Buckingham Palace Rd SW1. 01-930 4832. The home of the royal carriage horses and the royal carriages. Among the more discreet landaus, and even motor cars, are the gold State Coach used since the time of George III, for whom it was made, the pretty Irish State Coach, and the Glass Coach, used for royal weddings. *Open 14.00–16.00 Wed & Thur. Closed during Royal Ascot week.* Charge.

Royalty and Empire
Windsor and Eton Central Railway Station, High St, Windsor, Berks. (0753) 857837. The occasion is Queen Victoria's Diamond Jubilee. The Tussaud's life-size models recreate the moment when the queen met European members of the Royal Family at this very station to conduct them to Windsor Castle for the festivities. There stands the carriage, the horses, the waiting guards, the queen and other royals, with a background of stirring music. There is also an hourly film show which uses computer technology to bring eminent Victorian figures to life, and a small exhibition of a few of the Queen's possessions. *Open all year 09.30–17.00 Mon–Sun.* Charge.

Tower of London   15 M 10
Tower Hill EC3. 01-709 0765. London's oldest and most popular museum – the armouries have been inspiring awe in visitors since the time of Elizabeth I. Begun by William the Conqueror, added to by many later sovereigns, it is still designated a Royal Palace, and was a royal residence until the time of James I. It can almost be regarded as a group of museums, around which Yeomen Warders (Beefeaters) lead optional conducted tours.

The White Tower Has the largest and finest collection of medieval, Tudor, and 17thC armour in Britain and also houses Britain's oldest church, the Norman Chapel of St John

The Bloody Tower Has two rooms furnished as they would have been during Sir Walter Raleigh's 12-year incarceration.

The Beauchamp Tower Has inscriptions carved by state prisoners.

The Bowyer Tower Has grisly instruments of torture and the executioner's block and axe.

The Oriental Gallery Has armour for horse, elephant and Samurai.

The Herald's Museum Has coats of arms and heraldic banner devices.
The History Gallery Tells the story of the development of the Tower itself.
Chapel Royal of St Peter Ad Vincula The 16thC chapel, dedicated to St Peter in Chains, has some unmarked royal burials.
The Fusiliers' Museum Weapons and insignia of the Royal Fusiliers.

The Crown Jewels
The Crown Jewels, or Regalia, mostly date from after the Restoration of the monarchy in 1660. They are kept in the Jewel Tower of the Tower of London, under both traditional and modern electronic security. They include the Ampulla (14th century) and Spoon (12th century) for anointing the Sovereign during the coronation ceremony; St Edward's Crown – also used for Coronations – made for Charles II and named after Edward the Confessor; Victoria's Crown of State, with its great ruby, used both for coronations and state occasions; the orb, ring and two sceptres, one bearing one of the four 'Stars of Africa', a 530-carat diamond; and the Crown of Queen Elizabeth, now Queen Mother, set with the famous Koh-i-Noor diamond from India.

The Jewel House Has the Crown Jewels, Royal Regalia and Royal Plate. *Open 09.30–17.00 Mon–Sat (to 16.00 winter); 14.00–17.00 Sun. Closed Sun in winter & Nat Hols.* Charge. Extra charge for Jewel House.

Victoria & Albert Museum   19 H 3 Cromwell Rd SW7. 01-589 6371. The foundation stone for the present building was laid by Queen Victoria in 1899, on the site of the earlier Museum of Ornamental Art (also opened by Her Majesty in 1857), on land bought at the encouragement of Prince Albert and with the proceeds of the Great Exhibition. The queen chose the name for the museum, and in 1909 it was opened by Edward VII. Victoria and Albert preside over the entrance in effigy.

The structure is one of the most extravagant pieces of Victorian architecture in London and contains a wonderfully rich collection of decorative and applied arts from all categories and most countries and centuries. There are extensive and choice examples of paintings, sculpture, graphics, prints and drawings, typography, armour and weapons; carpets, ceramics, clocks, costume, fabrics, furniture, jewellery, metalwork and musical instruments, displayed in more than 10 acres of museum space set around an Italianate Garden, the latter designed in 1986 and opened in 1987. *Open 10.00–17.50 Mon–Thur & Sat; 14.30–17.50 Sun. Closed Fri & some Nat Hols.* Optional charge.

THEATRES, CINEMAS & CONCERT HALLS

Members of the Royal Family have attended film premieres, theatre performances and concerts in many venues in London, but the following have specific royal connections of one sort or another.

Performance details appear in the national press, *Time Out* and *City Limits*. Seats may be booked at the relevant box office, or through a ticket agency who will charge a fee.

The best known of the ticket agencies, Keith Prowse, with branches throughout London including in major hotels and stores, is By Appointment to the Queen Mother.

London Palladium   13 A 6 8 Argyll St W1. 01-437 7373. The site of a circus which became the setting for spectacular reviews in the lavish music-hall building of 1910. It was for some years the venue for the Royal Command Variety Performance, until Drury Lane took over. Pantomimes and variety shows still predominate. Bars.

Odeon Leicester Square   13 G 10 Leicester Sq W2. 01-930 6111. Large and well-appointed cinema which is almost invariably the setting for the Royal Film Performance, attended alternate years by the Queen and the Queen Mother.

Queen Elizabeth Hall &   14 O 13 Purcell Room South Bank SE1. 01-928 3191. There is seating for 1,100 at the Queen Elizabeth Hall which shares its foyer with the Purcell Room and uses its larger space for symphony, orchestral and big band concerts. It also stages some special events such as film shows and Poetry International. The Purcell Room, with seating for 372, is ideal for chamber music and solo concerts. The halls were opened by the Queen on 1st March 1967. Bar and coffee bar in the shared foyer and all the facilities of the Royal Festival Hall near at hand.

Royal Academy of   **5 C 15**
Dramatic Art
62 Gower St WC1. 01-580 7982. Britain's premiere drama school was founded by Sir Herbert Beerbohm Tree in 1904 and the Royal Charter was granted in 1920. It has three theatres, the proscenium-arched Vanbrugh in Malet Street, opened by the Queen Mother in 1954; the flexible George Bernard Shaw and the tiny Studio 13, both in Gower Street. Experimental plays and revivals get the full production treatment and RADA students take their finals in front of an audience. *Send sae for performance and booking details.*

Royal Academy of Music   **4 S 19**
Marylebone Rd NW1. 01-935 5461. England's oldest such institution, founded in 1823 under the patronage of George IV. A Royal Charter was granted in 1830. The present premises include a concert hall and a small theatre, and members of the public may book for the varied concerts given by advanced students throughout the year. Write or telephone for the *Diary of Events.*

Royal Albert Hall   **11 E 19**
Kensington Gore SW7. 01-589 8212. On a site bought, at the suggestion of Prince Albert, with the proceeds from the Great Exhibition. Queen Victoria laid the foundation stone in 1868, after Albert's death, and the Prince of Wales opened the hall in 1870.

Eighty visiting royals enjoyed the Shakespeare Ball here in 1911, and coronation balls were held in 1937 and 1953. Perhaps best known for the summer 'Prom' concerts, though all year there are orchestral, choral, rock and pop concerts (despite the fact that musicians dislike the acoustics, especially the persistent echo). Also a venue for sporting events and large meetings. There are bars for sandwiches and drinks. A recently introduced guided tour includes views of the amphitheatre from a private box and the Queen's Box regally dressed for a gala concert.

Royal College of Music   **11 E 20**
Prince Consort Rd SW7. 01-589 3643. Founded in 1882 by Edward, Prince of Wales and incorporated by Royal Charter in 1883. A fixture list is published at the start of each term, giving details of the chamber, orchestral and choral concerts and operas put on by students in their opera theatre, concert hall and recital hall. Standards are high and it's free – no refreshments (no room). Also has a museum of nearly 500 keyboard, wind and stringed instruments dating from the 16th to the 19th centuries, *Open Mon & Wed, and a Department of Portraits which is open by appointment only.*

Royal Festival Hall   **14 O 14**
South Bank SE1. 01-928 3191. Built for the Festival of Britain in 1951, the concert hall, with seating for 3,000 people, stages orchestral and choral concerts. The foyers have exhibitions as well as bars, a restaurant, a salt beef bar, salad bar, pasta bar, wine and coffee bars. There are also occasional film and ballet performances. The Royal Box is designed to give the public a good view of visiting royal patrons and behind the scenes there is even a loo specially for royalty. The guided tour usually at *12.45 & 17.30 Mon–Sun* is recommended.

Royal Opera House   **13 L 8**
Floral St WC2. 01-240 1066. This splendid construction by E. M. Barry is the third theatre of the same name on the site. More familiarly referred to by its audiences as Covent Garden, it is home to the Royal Opera Company – founded as the Covent Garden Opera Company in 1946 – and the Royal Ballet Company who were based at Sadler's Wells until 1956. It is England's foremost opera house where you will see the great names of opera and ballet in a suitably lavish setting. The mailing list brings priority booking with discounts, or it is possible to queue outside for cheap, same day tickets. Bars for drinks and snacks and light suppers in the Crush Bar.

There is a Royal Box and royal patrons have a withdrawing room where food is brought and served to them by their own staff. They also have the use of the King's Smoking Room. Named after Albert, Prince of Wales (Edward VII), this chamber was decorated in Wedgwood blue to match the interior of the Royal Yacht. During the Prince's time, a small door led from the King's Smoking Room directly to the stage so that the actresses could entertain him privately.

Theatre Royal, Drury Lane   **14 N 8**
Catherine St WC2. 01-836 8108. Usually known as 'Drury Lane', though in fact it's just around the corner. This glamorous, richly decorated, fourth theatre of the name on the site is now the regular venue for the Royal Command Variety Performance, attended alternate years by the Queen and the Queen Mother. The succeeding Royal Boxes have accommodated every reigning monarch since Charles II; indeed Nell Gwynne, one of Charles' many mistresses, performed here.

Here, too, attempts were made on the lives of George II and George III; and this is where William IV, when Duke of Clarence, first encountered his actress mistress Mrs Jordan. Well known for major musicals and for the best-loved of theatre ghosts, The Man In Grey.

Theatre Royal, Haymarket   **13 F 11**
Haymarket SW1. 01-930 9832. Founded early in the 18thC as 'the little theatre in the Hay', this one has come a long way, especially since it moved into the present building in the 1820s. It has been the setting for Royal Command performances in the past – in 1794 at the first such event, 15 people were crushed to death in the excitement. Plays of quality are presented here as befits the grand Palladian exterior created by Nash, and the gracious, gilded interior.

PUBS & RESTAURANTS

This section does not attempt to list every pub in London called The Queen's Head or The King's Head, because most of them do not have a real royal connection and some originally began trading as The Pope's Head and were only renamed during The Reformation. The younger Royals of today may occasionally be spotted at some of the capital's more exclusive and fashionable clubs and restaurants. Here are a few places with rather more specific royal associations.

Pub hours vary slightly but are usually 11.00–15.00 and 17.30–23.00 Mon–Sat; 12.00–14.00 and 19.00–22.30 Sun. Similarly, most restaurants open for two sessions a day – for lunch and dinner. These times apply below unless otherwise stated.

The Clifton   **3 A 7**
96 Clifton Hill NW8. 01-624 5233. Inside, all is Edwardiana and rightly so for here in the snug is where Lily Langtry and Edward VII used to rendezvous. Prints of the wayward king and Lily decorate the walls. China plates, stripped wood and three fireplaces give the pub a homely atmosphere. Varied and tasty bar meals available.

Gordon's Wine Cellar   **13 L 12**
47 Villiers St WC2. 01-930 1408. Three hundred-year-old cellar hidden in Watergate Walk whose proprietors have traded with royal sanctions as Free Vintners since the days of Edward III. Damp stone walls, candlelight, pleasant atmosphere; wines, sherries, ports and madeiras; cold buffet in summer, hot meals in winter. *Closes 21.00 & all Sat & Sun.*

Princess Louise   **14 P 3**
208 High Holborn WC1. 01-405 8816. Fine

Victorian pub of 1891 named after Queen Victoria's fourth daughter, a talented sculptor whose statue of her mother stands outside Kensington Palace. Its carefully preserved interior – all alterations in keeping with the original – good beer, jolly atmosphere and imaginative food combined to persuade *The London Evening Standard* to name it their Pub of the Year in 1986.

Queen's Elm   **19 F 10**
241 Fulham Rd SW3. 01-352 9157. Though the present pub only dates from 1914, it inherited its name from a previous hostelry on the site which in turn was called after a tree beneath which Queen Elizabeth I sheltered from the rain in 1567. The genial atmosphere is popular with local writers.

Rules Restaurant   **13 K 10**
35 Maiden Lane, WC2. 01-836 5314. A splendidly preserved slice of Edwardian London. Edward VII dined Lily Langtry in an upstairs room – and Thackeray and Dickens ate here, too. Electric chandeliers now, but authentic panelling, pictures and playbills. Roast beef or jugged hare are typical offerings. Booking essential. *Closed Sat & Sun.*

Ye Olde Mitre Tavern   **14 U 2**
1 Ely Pl EC1. 01-405 4751. The tavern was first built in 1546, by the bishops of Ely, to house their servants. Although rebuilt in the 18thC it still has its olde worlde charm – the bar broken up into small rooms with panelled walls and gentle lighting. The cherry tree preserved in the corner was once on the boundary between the lovely gardens of Sir Christopher Hatton, Elizabeth I's much-loved Chancellor, and the bishops' land. It is said that the queen once danced around the tree. Bar snacks available. *Closed Sat & Sun.*

THE RIVER THAMES

Today, although tourists, oarsmen and others may appreciate it, too many Londoners regard the river as no more than an irritating barrier dividing the capital. This river, however, which John Burns referred to as 'liquid history', is the reason for London's position, and for centuries it was an important highway. Mindful of this, monarchs built palaces near its banks and royal barges were used to travel between them. Not all the journeys were happy – sometimes the route led to The Tower, and Elizabeth I's funeral procession travelled on this waterway.

Annual events

There are several annual events on the river. One or two, such as the Oxford and Cambridge Boat Race, are quite famous; the following are those with royal interest.

Doggetts Coat & Badge Race 15 F 11
A rowing race for Thames Watermen between London Bridge and Chelsea, sometimes called 'The Watermen's Derby'. It was initiated by Thomas Doggett, theatre manager, in commemoration of the acces-

sion to the throne of George I, and he made the original provision, in his will, for the said coat to be made up, and badge attached, for the winner. *Takes place late Jul.*

Henley Royal Regatta

Held at Henley Reach, just over a mile and a quarter of straight river, upon which oarsmen compete for old-established trophies. It is also a highly social event, where striped blazers and straw boaters are the order of the day for the gentlemen; elegant dresses and hats for the ladies. Members of the Stewards' Enclosure and their guests are serenaded by the band of one of the Guards' regiments while they sip Pimms or champagne and occasionally watch the rowing. The Regatta was founded in 1839 but became Royal in 1851 when Prince Albert became its patron. *Takes place 1st week in Jul.*

Swan Upping

All the swans on the Thames are owned either by the Queen, whose birds remain unmarked, by the Worshipful Company of Vintners, whose birds have two nicks on their beaks, or the Worshipful Company of Dyers, whose birds have one nick. During the third week of July each year the swans hatched that spring must be marked and Her Majesty's Swankeeper and the Swan Markers of the two Companies work their way upriver from Blackfriars to Henley, rounding up the swans, marking them and pinioning them so that they don't leave the river. Traditional skiffs are used and special uniforms worn which makes the project into a colourful ceremony. *Takes place 3rd week in Jul.*

Barges & Bargemasters

Until 1919 each Sovereign had a Royal Barge and appointed a Bargemaster and Watermen. Nowadays the appointments are largely ceremonial, but the Bargemaster, in his red livery, and four Watermen attend the State Opening of Parliament in memory of the days when the monarch would have approached Westminster by water. They may also occasionally be in attendance when the Queen is present at some function connected with the river. Four of the City Livery Companies also have Bargemasters, each with his distinctive livery – the Vintners, the Fishmongers, the Watermen and the Dyers.

Royal landmarks along the river

ROYAL WINDSOR

Dominated by the 800-year-old medieval fortress of Windsor Castle. Of all the Royal Palaces, this is the one occupied most consistently – the Queen is in official residence here for at least a quarter of the year; at Christmas, for parts of March, April and May, in June for Royal Ascot week and also for the Garter Service in St George's Chapel, burial place of kings and queens for nearly 900 years.

Windsor Great Park, once a royal hunting ground, is almost entirely open to the public and contains the famous Safari Park.

Windsor received a Royal Charter in 1726; since 1974 its official title has been the Royal Borough of Windsor and Maidenhead. The town originally grew to house those who worked at the castle, but the coming of the railways opened it up to everyone.

Everywhere there are reminders of its royal associations. The three-mile Long Walk leads from the George IV Gateway of the castle up to The Copper Horse, an 1831 equestrian statue of George III; nearby is the Frogmore Mausoleum commissioned by Queen Victoria on the death of Prince Albert. The Victorian connections are particularly strong – Queen Victoria's statue dominates the centre of town and she appears in effigy at Madame Tussaud's Royalty and Empire exhibition at Central Station.

The State Apartments at Windsor Castle are frequently open to the public, as are The Royal Mews Exhibition and The Household Cavalry Museum. There is royal pageantry *daily at 10.30* when the Guard at the castle changes; the Royal Family attend the Royal Windsor Horse Show in the Home Park in July and are sometimes present at Windsor Racecourse and at Smiths' Lawn for polo. They have patronised the Theatre Royal for many years and the Queen usually takes her Ascot House Party to a production there in June.

Just the other side of the river stands the world-famous Eton College, founded by Henry VI in 1440.

HAMPTON COURT

This beautiful stretch of river is famous for the magnificent building and grounds of Hampton Court Palace, originally built by Cardinal Wolsey and given to Henry VIII in an unsuccessful attempt to regain favour. It has been a royal possession ever since.

Henry VIII lived in the palace with five of his wives; Jane Seymour died here giving birth to Edward VI and Catherine Howard was taken from here to her execution. The spirits of both queens are said to haunt the corridors. Elizabeth I spent much time here and took great practical interest in the gardens. James I and Charles I used the palace – in fact Charles was imprisoned here for a time after the Civil War. Charles II attended to repairing the palace and redesigned the gardens. William and Mary were responsible for extensions and modernisations; and there was further interior decoration carried out on the orders of Queen Anne, George I and George II, after which no British monarch actually lived here, though they cared for and maintained it. Queen Victoria opened the State Apartments to the public.

Hampton Court is best approached by river – in the manner of the early monarchs in their royal barges – and disembarking to explore the ornate and extensive gardens and the magnificent State Apartments is highly recommended.

RICHMOND

All that now remains of Richmond Palace is an old gateway on which the arms of Henry VII can just be recognised; but Richmond Park is royal – at one time a royal hunting ground and now a Royal Deer Park. The White Lodge, at present the base of the Royal Ballet School, was once a residence of Queen Caroline. Edward VII was born here and the Queen Mother and George VI lived in it when they were Duke and Duchess of York. Thatched House Lodge, also in the park, is currently home to Princess Alexandra and the Hon Angus Ogilvy.

The name of Richmond was brought to the area by Henry VII himself, who was formerly Earl of Richmond in Yorkshire. Richmond Hill is famous for its magnificent view of the Thames, best observed from The Terrace, and painted by Turner among other artists.

KEW

The Royal Botanic Gardens at Kew sweep down to the river and the beautiful trees and some of the outstanding features – such as the immensely high flagpole – are clearly visible from the water. It has had royal links since 1731 when the then Prince of Wales leased a house here and, like neighbouring Richmond, it became the chosen setting for homes of courtiers.

George II lived at Richmond Lodge in the gardens (the house no longer exits), and George III and Queen Charlotte lived in Kew Palace. A Royal Commission gave the gardens to the public in 1841.

CHELSEA

The Royal Borough of Kensington and Chelsea was formed in 1965 when the two were formally linked but its best known 'royal' landmark is the Royal Hospital which lies just north of Ranelagh Gardens, which in turn front on to Chelsea Embankment beside Chelsea Bridge.

The Royal Hospital is a unique retirement home founded by Charles II for aged and infirm soldiers – the Chelsea Pensioners – whose summertime uniform of 18thC scarlet frock coats and black tricorn hats dazzle visitors. (In winter, a more discreet navy is the form.)

The building, by Sir Christopher Wren, has a small museum and the grounds are the setting for the famous massed blooms of the Chelsea Flower Show each spring.

The Hospital is in fact the last of the Chelsea 'palaces' of the 16thC, grand houses built here by the gentry which earned the area the nickname 'village of palaces'.

WESTMINSTER

The great landmark at Westminster, majestically visible from the river, is the grand Gothic-style structure of the Houses of Parliament – more properly entitled the New Palace of Westminster – flanked by Big Ben, which is more correctly called St Stephen's Tower. Big Ben is the nickname of the great bell which hangs inside.

The Houses of Parliament stand on a site first occupied as a royal residence and seat of power by Edward the Confessor, and the present building still has the status of Royal Palace. Interestingly, though, by tradition the Sovereign is not allowed within the House of Commons and must open Parliament from the Lords.

The companion landmark, Westminster Abbey, magnificent repository of much of the royal history of England, has many royal tombs and has been the setting for coronations since 1066 and for most royal weddings. The land on which Westminster Abbey stands was once an island – Thorney Island – surrounded by marshes. A Benedictine Abbey was the first structure on the site, which in those days was rather remote, though equipped with a fresh water spring and good fishing in the Thames.

It is said that the 7thC King Sebert, the 8thC King Offa of Mercia, and the 10thC King Edgar all once owned the area, though there is no definite proof of this. Westminster's royal links from the time of Edward the Confessor are, however, undisputed.

THE TOWER OF LONDON

This grim and famous fortress looks deceptively pale and innocent from outside but its old river entrance – The Traitor's Gate – is a chilling reminder of its role as dungeon and death-cell as well as fortress, arsenal and museum.

The Traitor's Gate entrance is dry now, but when the river was a major arterial route through London many prisoners were brought to this entrance by barge, at the appropriate state of the tide. It was said that the water dragging out through the arch, as the tide went out, produced a frightening and depressing background anthem to the misery of the doomed prisoners within. Elizabeth I arrived by this route for her temporary internment when still a princess.

But not all river journeys associated with the Tower were wholly gloomy; Richard of Gloucester travelled from here by water to be crowned Richard III at Westminster. There was a shadow, though. He left behind the two young princes in the Garden

Tower, which was renamed The Bloody Tower after their murder a month or so later.

TOWER BRIDGE

The most famous, beautiful and theatrical of London's many river bridges had its foundation stone laid by the then Prince of Wales in 1881 and was officially opened by him in 1894.

GREENWICH

On a beautiful bend in the river stands Greenwich Park. This is one of the Royal Parks of London, and the present-day setting for the Royal Naval College, in its elegant Wren buildings, and for the National Maritime Museum, its two wings flanking the Queen's House, built by Inigo Jones for Anne of Denmark. On the hill behind stands the Old Royal Observatory, a group of buildings that includes the house once lived in by Flamsteed, the first Astronomer Royal.

Greenwich was the setting for a sumptuous Tudor palace. Henry VI, Henry VII and Henry VIII lived here, but it was Henry VIII, in particular, who favoured the palace and enjoyed sports and masques in its surrounding grounds. Elizabeth I and James I spent time here, and Charles II indulged in extensive rebuilding, but William and Mary eschewed it and shortly afterwards it was demolished.

THE ROYAL DOCKS

Little remains of Henry VIII's naval dockyard at Deptford, where the ships that repelled the Spanish Armada were built and where Sir Francis Drake was knighted by Elizabeth I on board the *Golden Hind*. The ship was kept here for years, in retirement, until it finally collapsed.

The last docks to be built in London were the royal group made up of the Royal Victoria, the Royal Albert and the King George V, together forming the world's largest wet dock (as opposed to dry docks used for repairs). They lie north of the river, at Silvertown, more or less opposite Woolwich.

The Victoria was opened by Prince Albert, the Royal Albert by the Duke of Connaught on behalf of Queen Victoria. The King George V was held back by World War I and not opened until 1921. In their day they were commercial and successful – now, like so much of London's Docklands, they bide their time, awaiting developments.

GUARDS & WARDERS

Although the Metropolitan Police protect the Queen and members of the Royal Family when they are in London, the Sovereign's more famous guardians are drawn from the ranks of the British Army. Although in one or two cases the duties are purely ceremonial, in the case of the guards the protection is genuine, despite the musical-comedy uniforms.

The Guards

Under the umbrella title of Household Division are five regiments of Foot Guards and two of Household Cavalry, all dedicated specifically to the protection of the Sovereign. It is in their glamorous ceremonial dress that they are best known to the public, because it is during their ceremonial duties that most people see them, but they are also fighting men, equipped with combat uniforms, who serve in Northern Ireland, the Falklands or wherever the British Army requires.

The Foot Guards

These are made up of five regiments, the Grenadiers, the Coldstreams, the Scots, Irish and Welsh. These are the men who, among other duties, stand guard at Buckingham Palace, and they are such a familiar sight, in scarlet tunics and black bearskins, that they may all look alike, but the differences in uniform are not hard to spot.

The Grenadier Guards wear white plumes in their bearskins and the buttons on their tunics are evenly spaced.

The Coldstream Guards have red plumes and buttons arranged in pairs.

The Scots Guards wear no plumes and their buttons are grouped in threes.

The Irish Guards wear blue plumes and their buttons are grouped in fours.

The Welsh Guards wear white and green plumes and have their buttons grouped in fives.

The Household Cavalry

The Household Cavalry is made up of the Life Guards and the Blues and Royals. They are based at Knightsbridge Barracks and can often be seen exercising their magnificent black horses early in the morning in Hyde Park, and mount guard at Horse Guards Parade in Whitehall.

Their ceremonial uniform of plumed helmet, cuirass (a kind of all-round breastplate), white buckskin breeches, thigh-high black boots and gauntlets makes that of the Foot Guards look distinctly pedestrian.

It is easy to recognise the difference between the Life Guards, who have white plumes in their helmets and red tunics, and the Blues and Royals who have red plumes and blue tunics.

Gentlemen at Arms
The Sovereign's Bodyguard of the Honourable Corps of the Gentlemen at Arms has its HQ at St James's Palace and each member – an officer of distinction in the British Army or Royal Marines – takes a special oath of allegiance to the Sovereign. Founded by Henry VIII, their duties are now largely ceremonial. They are responsible, for example, for very discreet 'crowd control' at the royal garden parties.

The Yeomen of the Guard
The Queen's Bodyguard of the Yeomen of the Guard are the oldest military corps in existence and are not to be confused with the Yeomen Warders of the Tower, despite the similarity of the Tudor uniforms. They were founded by Henry VII, their HQ is in St James's Palace, and they are recruited from retired senior non-commissioned officers of the British Army, RAF and Royal Marines. They attend the Queen at investitures and have to search the cellars before she opens Parliament.

Yeomen Warders of the Tower
Founded by Edward VI, and dressed in distinctive ceremonial Tudor uniforms, these are the famous Beefeaters. They are retired non-commissioned army officers whose principal duties now are to guide tourists around the huge and historic fortress and to perform the ancient Ceremony of the Keys, when the Tower is symbolically locked for the night.

HERALDRY

The now elaborate science of heraldry began in medieval times when personal symbols were used as a means of identification on the field of battle. Royal Coats of Arms, and those of ancient families, are the best known, but armorial bearings can also be granted to civic bodies and institutions.

Royal Coats of Arms

Each member of the Royal Family has his or her own coat of arms – the Sovereign grants arms to all the children of the extended Royal Family at a suitable age – but the four most frequently met with in London are those of the Queen, the Queen Mother, the Duke of Edinburgh and the Prince of Wales, since these are displayed to show that a shop or other establishment holds a Royal Warrant for its services.

College of Arms   *14 Y   8*
Queen Victoria St EC4. 01-248 2762. Housed in a discreet brick building of 1671, the College of Arms, which is under the authority of the Sovereign, is headed by the Earl Marshal, whose office is hereditary in the family of the Duke of Norfolk. Beneath the Earl Marshal are 13 officers. The College arranges matters ceremonial and heraldic, grants and devises arms, considers genealogical claims and stores the official records of English and Welsh genealogy. *Not open to the general public.*

The Queen's Beasts

Ten heraldic creatures inherited by the Queen – the originals are in the Great Hall at Hampton Court Palace. Plaster models sculpted by James Woodford RA were used to decorate Westminster Abbey at the Coronation in 1953, and Portland stone replicas of these coronation models now guard the palm houses in Kew Gardens.

The 10 creatures are: the Lion of England, who carries the Royal Arms; the Griffin of Edward III who carries the arms of the House of Windsor; the Falcon of the Plantagenets; the Black Bull of Clarence; the White Lion of Mortimer; the Yale of Beaufort, a mythical beast whose horns point in opposite directions and which is an heraldic rarity; the White Greyhound of Richmond; the Red Dragon of Wales; the Unicorn of Scotland; and the White Horse of Hanover which came with George I.

The Royal Standard

The Royal Standard, (with the three lions of England in the first and fourth quarters, the lion of Scotland in the second, and the harp of Ireland in the third), is personal to the Sovereign and is flown to indicate that she is in residence at a Royal Palace, a Royal House or on the Royal Yacht. It also flies on the royal car on official journeys and on the royal plane when it stands on the ground. The Royal Standard is never flown at half-mast.

The Union Jack
The British national flag is formed by the union of three heraldic flags – the red cross of St George, the white saltire (X-shaped) cross of St Andrew surmounted by the red saltire cross of St Patrick. The crosses appear against the blue background of St Andrew's banner.

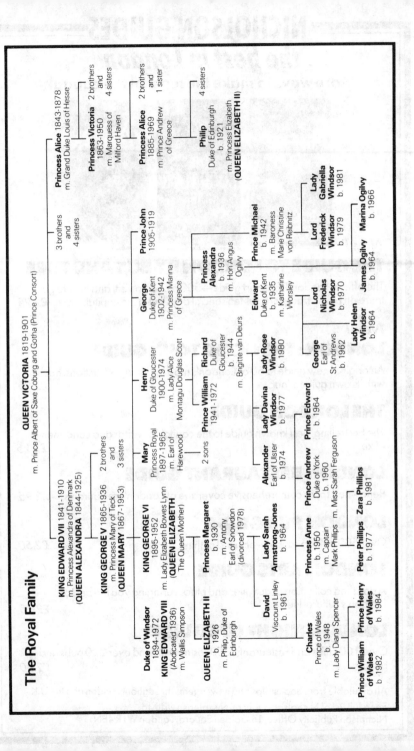

The Royal Family

QUEEN VICTORIA 1819-1901
m. Prince Albert of Saxe Coburg and Gotha (Prince Consort)

KING EDWARD VII 1841-1910
m. Princess Alexandra of Denmark
(QUEEN ALEXANDRA 1844-1925)

3 brothers and 4 sisters

Princess Alice 1843-1878
m. Grand Duke Louis of Hesse

Princess Victoria 1863-1950
m. Marquess of Milford Haven

2 brothers and 4 sisters

Princess Alice 1885-1969
m. Prince Andrew of Greece

2 brothers and 1 sister

Philip
Duke of Edinburgh
b. 1921
m. Princess Elizabeth
(QUEEN ELIZABETH II)

4 sisters

KING GEORGE V 1865-1936
m. Princess Mary of Teck
(QUEEN MARY 1867-1953)

2 brothers and 3 sisters

Duke of Windsor
1894-1972
KING EDWARD VIII
(Abdicated 1936)
m. Wallis Simpson

KING GEORGE VI
1895-1952
m. Lady Elizabeth Bowes Lyon
(QUEEN ELIZABETH
The Queen Mother)

Mary
Princess Royal 1897-1965
m. Earl of Harewood

2 sons

Henry
Duke of Gloucester
1900-1974
m. Lady Alice
Montagu Douglas Scott

George
Duke of Kent
1902-1942
m. Princess Marina
of Greece

Prince John
1905-1919

QUEEN ELIZABETH II
b. 1926
m. Philip, Duke of Edinburgh

Princess Margaret
b. 1930
m. Antony
Earl of Snowdon
(divorced 1978)

Prince William
1941-1972

Richard
Duke of Gloucester
b. 1944
m. Brigitte van Deurs

Edward
Duke of Kent
b. 1935
m. Katharine Worsley

Princess Alexandra
b. 1936
m. Hon Angus Ogilvy

Prince Michael
b. 1942
m. Baroness
Marie Christine
von Reibnitz

David
Viscount Linley
b. 1961

Lady Sarah Armstrong-Jones
b. 1964

Alexander
Earl of Ulster
b. 1974

Lady Davina Windsor
b. 1977

Lady Rose Windsor
b. 1980

George
Earl of St Andrews
b. 1962

Lady Helen Windsor
b. 1964

Lord Nicholas Windsor
b. 1970

James Ogilvy
b. 1964

Marina Ogilvy
b. 1966

Lord Frederick Windsor
b. 1979

Lady Gabriella Windsor
b. 1981

Princess Anne
b. 1950
m. Captain
Mark Phillips

Prince Andrew
Duke of York
b. 1960
m. Miss Sarah Ferguson

Prince Edward
b. 1964

Charles
Prince of Wales
b. 1948
m. Lady Diana Spencer

Peter Phillips
b. 1977

Zara Phillips
b. 1981

Prince William
of Wales
b. 1982

Prince Henry
of Wales
b. 1984

18 Z 7 Colebeck ms SW5	18 U 2 Cope pl W8	14 U 5 Crane st EC4
6 X 7 Colebrooke row N1	6 S 6 Copenhagen st N1	5 C 9 Cranleigh st NW1
18 Y 12 Coleherne ms SW10	5 L 5 Copenhagen st N1	19 D 9 Cranley gdns SW7
18 X 11 Coleherne rd SW10	6 Z 4 Copford wlk N1	19 D 9 Cranley ms SW7
7 B 4 Coleman fields N1	7 A 3 Copford wlk N1	19 F 7 Cranley pl SW7
23 K 18 Coleman rd SE5	14 Z 16 Copperfield st SE1	22 U 18 Cranmer rd SW9
23 H 17 Coleman rd SE5	15 A 16 Copperfield st SE1	24 Y 10 Cranswick rd SE16
15 E 5 Coleman st EC2	13 J 2 Coptic st WC1	7 F 14 Cranwood st EC1
3 B 2 Coleridge gdns NW6	14 T 18 Coral st SE1	11 C 9 Craven Hill gdn W2
17 H 7 Colet gdns W14	5 J 17 Coram st WC1	11 C 8 Craven Hill ms W2
6 P 17 Coley st WC1	8 O 19 Corbet pl E1	11 D 8 Craven hill W2
6 V 1 College cross N1	8 X 7 Corbridge cres E2	13 K 12 Craven pas WC2
5 D 5 College gro NW1	8 X 15 Corfield st E2	11 D 7 Craven rd W2
5 C 4 College pl NW1	13 A 10 Cork St ms W1	13 K 12 Craven st WC2
1 B 8 College rd NW10	13 A 10 Cork st W1	11 D 8 Craven ter W2
24 U 2 Collett rd SE16	11 J 1 Corlett st NW1	12 O 1 Crawford ms W1
6 N 9 Collier st N1	15 G 6 Cornhill EC3	6 T 17 Crawford pas EC1
18 Z 7 Collingham gdns SW5	9 L 7 Cornwall cres W11	11 L 3 Crawford pl W1
18 Y 6 Collingham pl SW5	18 Z 3 Cornwall gdns SW7	12 N 2 Crawford st W1
8 X 17 Collingwood st E1	19 A 3 Cornwall gdns SW7	23 K 3 Creasy est SE1
6 X 5 Collins yd N1	18 Y 3 Cornwall gdns wlk SW7	1 E 6 Crediton rd NW10
15 A 19 Collinson st SE1	19 A 3 Cornwall Ms south SW7	24 Y 10 Credon rd SE16
8 R 16 Colman clo E2	18 X 2 Cornwall Ms west SW7	15 L 6 Creechurch la EC3
22 W 2 Colnbrook st SE1	14 T 14 Cornwall rd SE1	15 L 6 Creechurch pl EC3
14 W 15 Colombo st SE1	16 X 8 Cornwall st E1	14 Y 6 Creed la EC4
5 K 18 Colonnade WC1	4 S 18 Cornwall ter NW1	17 J 16 Crefeld clo W6
4 Y 15 Colosseum ter NW1	7 J 13 Coronet st N1	1 H 8 Creighton rd NW6
8 P 12 Columbia rd E2	6 U 16 Corporation row EC1	7 M 10 Cremer st E2
10 P 6 Colville gdns W11	7 G 13 Corsham st N1	19 G 16 Cremorne est SW10
10 R 6 Colville ms W11	5 L 20 Cosmo pl WC1	19 D 20 Cremorne gdns SW10
13 D 2 Colville pl W1	22 S 2 Cosser st SE1	19 E 19 Cremorne st SW10
10 P 5 Colville rd W11	3 L 20 Cosway st NW1	19 L 5 Crescent pl SW3
10 R 7 Colville rd W11	23 C 7 Cotham st SE17	7 A 17 Crescent row EC1
10 O 5 Colville Sq ms W11	23 H 18 Cottage grn SE5	16 N 9 Crescent the EC3
10 O 6 Colville sq W11	19 J 2 Cottage pl SW3	19 B 9 Cresswell gdns SW5
10 P 6 Colville ter W11	18 Z 1 Cottesmore gdns W8	19 C 10 Cresswell pl SW10
17 E 14 Colwith rd W6	19 A 1 Cottesmore gdns W8	5 K 12 Crestfield st WC1
23 B 8 Colworth gro SE17	22 V 9 Cottington st SE11	22 S 19 Crewdson rd SW9
23 B 20 Comber gro SE5	7 M 12 Cottons gdns E2	22 X 7 Cricketers ct SE11
17 M 10 Comeragh ms W14	20 O 8 Coulson st SW3	23 L 3 Crimscott st SE1
18 N 10 Comeragh rd W14	17 A 2 Coulter rd W6	21 F 20 Crimsworth rd SW8
17 L 11 Comeragh rd W14	23 A 20 Councillor st SE5	5 L 7 Crinan st N1
16 U 5 Commercial rd E1	15 E 15 Counter ct SE1	21 C 17 Cringle st SW8
16 O 2 Commercial st E1	23 D 3 County st SE1	17 C 11 Crisp rd W6
23 M 20 Commercial way SE15	23 C 3 County st SE1	15 M 1 Crispin st E1
24 T 18 Commercial way SE15	22 S 10 Courtenay sq SE11	16 R 10 Crofts st E1
10 S 20 Commonwealth institute W8	22 S 10 Courtenay st SE11	5 K 14 Cromer st WC1
4 Z 14 Compton clo NW1	18 Z 6 Courtfield gdns SW5	3 E 19 Crompton st W2
5 K 15 Compton pl WC1	18 Y 6 Courtfield gdns SW5	18 S 5 Cromwell cres W8
1 G 13 Compton rd NW10	19 A 6 Courtfield rd SW7	19 H 4 Cromwell gdns SW7
6 X 16 Compton st EC1	10 S 5 Courtnell st W2	9 D 20 Cromwell gro W6
23 H 6 Comus pl SE17	13 L 8 Covent gdn WC2	19 F 5 Cromwell ms SW7
14 P 14 Concert Hall appr SE1	10 N 6 Covent gdns W11	19 G 4 Cromwell pl SW7
13 K 8 Conduit ct WC2	2 V 7 Coventry clo NW6	18 X 5 Cromwell pl SW5
11 F 7 Conduit ms W2	8 Y 17 Coventry rd E1	19 C 5 Cromwell rd SW7
11 F 6 Conduit pas W2	8 Y 15 Coventry rd E1	7 J 10 Crondall st N1
11 G 6 Conduit pl W2	13 E 10 Coventry st W1	7 E 10 Cropley st N1
13 A 8 Conduit st W1	9 A 16 Coverdale rd W12	15 F 18 Crosby row SE1
12 Z 9 Conduit st W1	8 T 20 Coverley clo E1	15 J 5 Crosby sq EC3
23 J 7 Congreve st SE17	23 J 13 Cowan st SE5	12 U 2 Cross Keys clo W1
1 L 17 Conlan st W10	6 X 20 Cowcross st EC1	15 K 10 Cross la EC3
11 L 7 Connaught clo W2	6 N 3 Cowdenbeath pth N1	6 Y 3 Cross st N1
12 N 7 Connaught ms W2	22 U 20 Cowley rd SW14	15 M 8 Crosswall EC3
12 N 7 Connaught pl W2	21 J 1 Cowley st SW1	16 N 7 Crosswall EC3
12 N 6 Connaught sq W2	7 G 15 Cowper st EC2	8 U 3 Croston st E8
11 M 6 Connaught st W2	9 F 2 Cowper ter W10	16 W 9 Crowder st E1
11 M 6 Connaught sw W2	14 Z 3 Coxs ct EC1	13 M 7 Crown ct WC2
14 U 16 Cons st SE1	16 N 18 Coxson pl SE1	14 T 8 Crown Office row EC4
12 Y 17 Constitution hill SW1	17 F 17 Crabtree la SW6	13 C 14 Crown pas SW1
23 C 7 Content st SE17	13 J 13 Craigs ct SW1	23 B 18 Crown st SE5
5 A 18 Conway st W1	23 F 6 Crail row SE17	5 B 8 Crowndale rd NW1
22 V 14 Cooks rd SE17	13 H 9 Crambourne st WC2	2 R 13 Croxley rd W9
2 O 15 Coomassie rd W9	12 U 2 Cramer st W1	2 P 16 Croyton pth SW8
6 Y 10 Coombs st N1	22 Z 8 Crampton st SE17	15 K 17 Crucifix la SE1
5 G 9 Coopers la NW1	22 Z 7 Crampton st SE17	6 Y 6 Cruden st N1
24 P 10 Coopers rd SE1	8 T 18 Cranberry st E1	6 R 11 Cruikshank st WC1
15 M 8 Coopers row EC3	13 H 9 Cranbourne all WC2	15 L 8 Crutched Friars EC3
		6 O 14 Cubitt st WC1
		8 X 16 Cudworth st E1
		20 O 7 Culford gdns SW3
		7 J 2 Culford rd N1

23 A 13	Draco st SE17	
19 K 6	Draycott av SW3	
20 N 7	Draycott av SW3	
20 N 7	Draycott pl SW3	
20 O 6	Draycott ter SW3	
2 P 16	Drayford clo W9	
10 V 18	Drayson mews W8	
19 B 9	Drayton gdns SW10	
1 M 15	Droop st W10	
1 J 14	Droop st W10	
24 Y 17	Drover la SE15	
15 L 16	Druid st SE1	
16 O 19	Druid st SE1	
5 E 12	Drummond cres NW1	
21 F 10	Drummond ga SW1	
24 W 1	Drummond rd SE16	
16 W 20	Drummond rd SE16	
5 C 14	Drummond st NW1	
13 L 5	Drury la WC2	
22 U 7	Dryden Ct Housing est SE11	
22 V 6	Dryden ct SE11	
13 L 6	Dryden st WC2	
7 L 13	Drysdale st N1	
9 A 5	Du Cane rd W12	
8 P 14	Ducat st E2	
12 X 2	Duchess ms W1	
10 T 18	Duchess of Bedford's wlk W8	
12 Y 2	Duchess st W1	
14 T 12	Duchy st SE1	
13 D 7	Duck la W1	
2 N 8	Dudley rd NW6	
11 F 2	Dudley st W2	
11 F 2	Dudley st W2	
19 H 9	Dudmaston ms SW3	
7 D 17	Dufferin av EC1	
7 D 18	Dufferin st EC1	
13 C 7	Dufours pl W1	
12 V 17	Duke of Wellington pl SW1	
13 D 12	Duke of York st SW1	
15 G 13	Duke St hill SE1	
13 C 12	Duke st St James SW1	
10 V 17	Dukes la W8	
12 U 4	Dukes ms W1	
15 M 6	Dukes pl EC3	
5 G 14	Dukes rd WC1	
12 U 7	Duke st W1	
9 J 8	Dulford st W11	
4 T 1	Dumpton pl NW1	
8 V 16	Dunbridge st E2	
8 V 4	Duncan rd E8	
8 V 8	Duncan st N1	
6 W 9	Duncan ter N1	
13 J 11	Duncannon st WC2	
16 X 15	Dundee st E1	
16 K 9	Dundela gdns Worc Pk	
1 F 6	Dundonald rd NW10	
16 S 1	Dunk st E1	
7 M 9	Dunloe st E2	
8 P 9	Dunloe st E2	
24 P 3	Dunlop pl SE16	
1 K 5	Dunmore rd NW6	
7 A 3	Dunmow wlk N1	
12 S 8	Dunraven st W1	
17 E 3	Dunsany rd W14	
4 V 20	Dunstable ms W1	
2 P 1	Dunster gdns NW6	
8 N 5	Dunston rd E8	
7 M 4	Dunston st E8	
24 O 5	Dunton rd SE1	
23 M 8	Dunton rd SE1	
12 R 18	Duplex ride SW1	
8 S 11	Durant st E2	
13 L 11	Durham Ho st WC2	
20 O 11	Durham pl SW3	
22 O 12	Durham st SE11	
10 W 4	Durham ter W2	

16 V 1	Durward st E1	
8 W 20	Durward st E1	
12 R 1	Durweston ms W1	
12 P 1	Durweston st W1	
14 T 3	Dyers bldgs EC1	
2 N 1	Dyne rd NW6	
13 H 3	Dyott st WC1	
7 H 19	Dysart st EC2	

E

6 W 20	Eagle ct EC1	
14 O 2	Eagle st WC1	
7 D 7	Eagle Wharf rd N1	
3 L 9	Eamont st NW8	
18 U 11	Eardley cres SW5	
24 N 9	Earl cotts SE1	
24 N 9	Earl rd SE1	
7 H 20	Earl st EC2	
13 J 6	Earlham st WC2	
18 T 10	Earls Ct Exhibition bldg SW5	
18 X 7	Earls Ct gdns SW5	
18 T 2	Earls Ct rd W8	
18 W 10	Earls Ct sq SW5	
18 R 3	Earls ter W8	
18 T 3	Earls wlk W8	
5 M 3	Earlsferry way N1	
1 A 11	Earlsmead rd NW10	
6 W 13	Earlstoke st EC1	
8 Y 5	Earlston gro E9	
4 X 3	Early ms NW1	
13 H 4	Earnshaw ct WC2	
17 M 5	Earsby st W14	
12 V 4	Easleys ms W1	
14 U 5	East Harding st EC4	
16 S 20	East la SE16	
16 X 1	East Mount st E1	
14 Z 1	East pas EC1	
14 X 1	East Poultry av EC1	
7 F 12	East rd N1	
1 L 17	East row W10	
16 R 11	East Smithfield E1	
23 K 7	East st SE17	
23 G 8	East st SE17	
23 C 10	East st SE17	
24 N 19	East Surrey gro SE15	
16 P 6	East Tenter st E1	
11 D 5	Eastbourne ms W2	
11 D 5	Eastbourne ter W2	
13 C 4	Eastcastle st W1	
15 H 9	Eastcheap EC3	
6 S 15	Easton st WC1	
20 T 6	Eaton clo SW1	
20 V 3	Eaton gate SW1	
20 Y 2	Eaton la SW1	
20 U 3	Eaton Ms north SW1	
20 V 4	Eaton Ms south SW1	
20 U 5	Eaton Ms west SW1	
20 U 3	Eaton pl SW1	
20 W 2	Eaton row SW1	
20 U 3	Eaton sq SW1	
20 T 5	Eaton Ter ms SW1	
20 S 5	Eaton ter SW1	
20 T 6	Eaton ter SW1	
22 O 15	Ebbisham drive SE11	
7 E 13	Ebenezer st N1	
23 L 15	Ebley clo SE15	
7 M 16	Ebor st E2	
20 V 11	Ebury Br rd SW1	
20 W 9	Ebury br SW1	
20 W 4	Ebury Ms east SW1	
20 W 5	Ebury ms SW1	
20 V 7	Ebury sq SW1	
20 V 6	Ebury st SW1	
7 B 2	Ecclesbourne rd N1	

20 Y 5	Eccleston br SW1	
20 V 2	Eccleston ms SW1	
20 W 6	Eccleston pl SW1	
20 Z 7	Eccleston Sq ms SW1	
20 Z 7	Eccleston sq SW1	
20 X 5	Eccleston st SW1	
8 R 18	Eckersley st E1	
6 R 7	Eckford st N1	
2 U 18	Edbrooke rd W9	
6 Z 4	Eder wlk N1	
10 U 14	Edge st WW8	
11 K 3	Edgware rd W2	
3 F 19	Edgware rd W2	
12 N 6	Edgware rd W2	
4 U 2	Edis st NW1	
18 N 8	Edith rd W14	
17 J 6	Edith rd W14	
8 R 7	Edith st E2	
18 B 17	Edith ter SW10	
18 O 8	Edith vlls W14	
23 F 18	Edmund st SE5	
6 N 6	Edward sq N1	
18 R 3	Edwardes sq W8	
12 T 6	Edwards ms W1	
12 T 6	Edwards ms W1	
6 N 6	Edwards sq N1	
18 U 19	Effie pl SW6	
18 U 19	Effie rd SW6	
24 W 10	Egan way SE16	
4 T 3	Egbert pl NW1	
4 T 2	Egbert st NW1	
19 L 4	Egerton cres SW3	
19 L 3	Egerton Gdns ms SW3	
1 C 5	Egerton gdns NW10	
19 K 4	Egerton gdns SW3	
19 L 3	Egerton pl SW3	
19 K 3	Egerton ter SW3	
23 C 5	Elba pl SE17	
19 L 19	Elcho st SW11	
24 V 18	Elcot av SE15	
7 M 19	Elder st E1	
19 A 2	Eldon rd W8	
18 Z 2	Eldon rd W8	
15 H 1	Eldon st EC2	
22 Y 3	Elephant and Castle SE1	
16 Z 17	Elephant la SE16	
23 A 4	Elephant rd SE17	
3 A 12	Elgin av W9	
2 T 17	Elgin av W9	
10 N 7	Elgin cres W11	
9 L 8	Elgin cres W11	
2 Z 12	Elgin Ms north W9	
3 A 13	Elgin Ms south W9	
9 M 5	Elgin ms W11	
6 W 10	Elia st N1	
22 S 16	Elias pl SE11	
7 D 2	Elizabeth av N1	
20 X 7	Elizabeth br SW1	
3 D 17	Elizabeth clo W9	
20 W 6	Elizabeth st SW1	
2 O 20	Elkstone rd W10	
17 F 15	Ellaline rd W6	
16 T 7	Ellen st E1	
22 W 20	Elliott rd SW9	
22 X 4	Elliotts row SE11	
20 R 4	Ellis st SW1	
8 X 12	Ellsworth st E2	
19 F 11	Elm Pk gdns SW10	
19 F 12	Elm Pk la SW3	
19 E 14	Elm Pk rd SW3	
19 F 10	Elm pl SW7	
6 P 17	Elm st WC1	
3 F 12	Elm Tree clo NW8	
3 F 13	Elm Tree rd NW8	
23 H 20	Elmington rd SE5	
23 E 20	Elmington rd SE5	
11 E 9	Elms ms W2	
2 Y 18	Elnathan ms W9	
9 K 19	Elsham rd W14	
23 G 8	Elsted st SE17	

12 N 7	Frederick clo W2
22 W 20	Frederick cres SW9
6 O 13	Frederick st WC1
7 M 2	Frederick ter E8
6 2	Freeling st N1
23 K 8	Freemantle SE17
8 Z 4	Fremont st E9
7 L 14	French pl E1
24 T 15	Frensham st SE15
9 F 9	Freston rd W11
14 X 7	Friar st EC4
14 X 19	Friars pl SE1
13 C 15	Friary ct SW1
24 U 18	Friary rd SE15
15 A 7	Friday st EC4
6 W 12	Friend st EC1
13 F 7	Frith st W1
9 B 13	Frithville gdns W12
7 A 7	Frome st N1
6 Z 7	Frome st N1
6 U 8	Fryes bldgs N1
15 M 2	Frying Pan all E1
16 Y 18	Fulford st SE16
18 T 18	Fulham bdy SW6
17 E 11	Fulham Palace rd W6
17 H 18	Fulham Palace rd SW6
19 G 9	Fulham rd SW3
18 T 19	Fulham rd SW6
7 G 11	Fullwood ms N1
11 A 9	Fulton ms W2
14 R 2	Fulwood pl WC1
24 T 20	Furley rd SE15
14 T 3	Furnival st EC4
21 F 5	Fynes st SW1

G

5 M 20	Gage st WC1
6 S 4	Gainford st N1
16 O 17	Gainsford st SE1
13 K 2	Galen pl WC1
8 Y 14	Gales gdns E8
24 W 6	Galley Wall rd SE16
1 K 15	Galton st W10
7 C 14	Galway st EC1
14 X 15	Gambia st SE1
13 B 7	Ganton st W1
12 U 1	Garbutt pl W1
6 Y 12	Gard st EC1
10 U 10	Garden ms W2
3 E 11	Garden rd NW8
22 X 2	Garden row SE1
7 J 15	Garden wlk EC2
15 C 9	Garlick hill EC4
6 T 13	Garnault ms EC1
6 U 14	Garnault pl EC1
16 Z 10	Garner st E1
8 U 9	Garner st E2
24 O 17	Garnies clo SE15
7 B 17	Garrett st EC1
13 J 9	Garrick st WC2
13 J 9	Garrick yd WC2
17 K 14	Garvan clo W6
10 W 7	Garway rd W2
8 N 12	Gascoigne pl E2
2 T 1	Gascony av NW6
22 R 12	Gasholder pl SE11
6 X 4	Gaskin st N1
17 H 13	Gastein rd W6
11 L 19	Gate ms SW7
14 N 3	Gate st WC2
3 J 17	Gateforth st NW8
7 J 16	Gatesborough st EC2
23 C 13	Gateway SE17
20 W 11	Gatliff rd SW1
23 G 6	Gavel st SE17

21 J 2	Gayfere st SW1
22 X 2	Gaywood st SE1
22 W 11	Gaza st SE17
16 O 12	Gedling pl SE1
6 Z 16	Gee st EC1
7 A 16	Gee st EC1
12 V 6	Gees ct W1
7 M 9	Geffrye museum E2
7 M 9	Geffrye st E2
24 W 19	Geldart rd SE15
19 G 3	Geological museum SW7
13 L 11	George ct WC2
15 F 15	George Inn yd SE1
16 S 19	George row SE16
12 T 3	George st W1
12 V 8	George yd W1
5 B 3	Georgiana st NW1
8 O 12	Georgina gdns E2
20 V 6	Gerald ms SW1
20 U 6	Gerald rd SW1
22 U 2	**GERALDINE MARY HARMSWORTH PARK SE11**
22 V 2	Geraldine st SE11
13 G 8	Gerrard pl W1
6 X 8	Gerrard rd N1
13 G 8	Gerrard st W1
14 U 20	Gerridge st SE1
19 D 15	Gertrude st SW10
24 Y 17	Gervase st SE15
18 P 9	Gibbs Green est W14
6 V 4	Gibson sq N1
17 K 9	Giddon rd W14
6 N 1	Gifford st N1
5 L 2	Gifford st N1
13 J 2	Gilbert pl WC1
22 V 6	Gilbert st SE11
12 V 7	Gilbert st W1
12 Z 2	Gildea st W1
20 Z 5	Gillingham ms SW1
21 A 5	Gillingham row SW1
21 A 5	Gillingham st SW1
20 Z 5	Gillingham st SW1
19 C 12	Gilston rd SW10
14 X 3	Giltspur st EC1
17 H 4	Girdlers rd W14
18 R 19	Gironde rd SW6
22 W 1	Gladstone st SE1
24 P 12	Glangall rd SE15
8 Y 15	Glass st E2
14 Y 18	Glasshill st SE1
13 C 10	Glasshouse st W1
21 M 9	Glasshouse wlk SE11
22 N 9	Glasshouse wlk SE11
17 L 9	Glazebury rd W14
19 J 13	Glebe pl SW3
19 A 8	Gledhow gdns SW5
17 L 11	Gledstanes rd W14
19 F 6	Glendower pl SW7
19 Y 18	Glenfinlas way
2 T 4	Glengall pass SW6
2 T 4	Glengall rd NW6
24 P 13	Glengall ter SE15
9 B 4	Glenroy st W12
17 A 6	Glenthorne rd W6
4 P 18	Glentworth st SW1
15 D 20	Globe st SE1
12 X 7	Globe yd W1
4 T 2	Gloucester av NW1
4 X 4	Gloucester cres NW1
4 W 7	Gloucester Ga ms NW1
4 W 7	Gloucester ga NW1
11 C 6	Gloucester Ms w W2
11 D 6	Gloucester ms W2
12 P 2	Gloucester Pl ms W1
4 O 18	Gloucester pl NW1

12 R 2	Gloucester pl W1
19 C 8	Gloucester rd SW7
21 B 8	Gloucester st SW1
11 H 7	Gloucester sw W2
11 C 6	Gloucester ter W2
6 U 10	Gloucester way EC1
10 U 16	Gloucester wlk W8
22 N 11	Glyn st SE11
19 M 3	Glynde ms SW3
16 N 16	Goat st SE1
18 P 19	Goaters all SW6
19 L 9	Godfrey st SW3
14 Z 7	Godliman st EC4
21 M 11	Godling st SE11
6 S 9	Godson st N1
2 N 19	Golborne gdns W10
9 L 1	Golborne ms W10
1 M 20	Golborne rd W10
9 L 1	Golborne rd W10
7 B 17	Golden la EC1
13 C 9	Golden sq W1
9 B 19	Goldhawk rd W12
2 Y 2	Goldhurst ter NW6
3 B 1	Goldhurst ter NW6
16 U 7	Golding st E1
5 E 7	Goldington cres NW1
5 F 8	Goldington st NW1
2 T 18	Goldney rd W9
16 U 5	Goldney ter E1
21 G 20	Goldsboro' rd SW8
8 T 9	Goldsmiths row E2
8 U 7	Goldsmiths sq E2
13 C 1	Goodge pl W1
13 D 1	Goodge st W1
16 R 6	Goodman st E1
16 O 8	Goodmans yd E1
5 J 8	Goods way NW1
13 J 9	Goodwins ct WC2
6 U 11	Goose yd EC1
7 G 6	Gopsall st N1
10 V 17	Gordon pl W8
5 F 17	Gordon sq WC1
5 E 16	Gordon st WC1
19 C 1	Gore st SW7
2 U 8	Gorefield pl NW6
9 J 11	Gorham pl W11
15 L 5	Goring st EC3
17 M 6	Gorleston st W14
8 N 11	Gorsuch pl E2
12 Z 1	Gosfield st W1
13 G 5	Goslett yd WC2
8 P 13	Gosset st E2
6 X 14	Goswell pl EC1
6 Y 15	Goswell rd EC1
14 U 5	Gough sq EC4
6 P 16	Gough st WC1
16 O 4	Goulston st E1
5 E 16	Gower ct WC1
13 F 1	Gower ms WC1
5 C 15	Gower st WC1
5 C 16	Gower st WC1
16 S 5	Gowers wlk E1
15 H 8	Gracechurch st EC3
16 T 9	Graces all E1
5 B 18	Grafton ms W1
5 F 13	Grafton pl NW1
12 Z 10	Grafton st W1
5 B 18	Grafton way W1
6 Z 10	Graham st N1
20 T 7	Graham ter SW1
23 F 6	Grail row SE17
22 N 7	Granby bldgs SE11
8 R 15	Granby st E2
5 A 10	Granby ter NW1
14 X 1	Grand av EC1
14 P 6	Grange ct WC2
23 L 2	Grange rd SE1
7 G 7	Grange st N1
23 M 1	Grange the SE1
24 N 1	Grange wlk SE1
23 L 2	Grange wlk SE1
24 N 2	Grange yd SE1

H

10 N 10	Lansdowne cres W11	
8 V 3	Lansdowne dri E8	
21 K 20	Lansdowne gdns SW8	
10 N 14	Lansdowne ms W11	
23 G 1	Lansdowne pl SE1	
10 N 12	Lansdowne rd W11	
9 M 9	Lansdowne rd W11	
9 M 10	Lansdowne ri W11	
12 Y 12	Lansdowne row W1	
5 M 17	Lansdowne ter WC1	
10 O 12	Lansdowne wlk W11	
15 A 18	Lant st SE1	
23 C 7	Larcom st SE17	
8 Z 6	Lark row E2	
9 C 4	Latimer pl W10	
9 D 5	Latimer rd W10	
24 R 15	Latona rd SE15	
22 N 10	Laud st SE11	
2 X 15	Lauderdale rd W9	
3 A 15	Lauderdale rd W9	
19 A 2	Launceston pl W8	
17 K 15	Laundry rd W6	
18 Y 8	Laverton ms SW5	
18 Y 7	Laverton pl SW5	
14 Z 14	Lavington st SE1	
5 M 8	Lavinia gro N1	
23 G 1	Law st SE1	
5 B 2	Lawfords wharf NW1	
22 N 15	Lawn la SW8	
21 M 14	Lawn la SW8	
5 L 4	Lawrence pl N1	
19 J 15	Lawrence st SW3	
22 Y 18	Laxley clo SE5	
4 Z 16	Laxton pl NW1	
24 X 4	Layard sq SE16	
6 S 18	Laystall st EC1	
6 U 7	Layton rd N1	
15 J 6	Leadenhall market EC3	
15 J 7	Leadenhall pl EC3	
15 K 6	Leadenhall st EC3	
14 R 18	Leake st SE1	
10 R 3	Leamington Rd vlls W11	
17 A 7	Leamore st W6	
14 T 2	Leather la EC1	
6 T 19	Leather la EC1	
15 H 18	Leathermarket st SE1	
19 F 10	Lecky st SW7	
10 T 7	Ledbury Ms north W11	
10 S 8	Ledbury Ms west W11	
10 S 7	Ledbury rd W11	
24 U 17	Ledbury st SE15	
7 M 3	Lee st E8	
8 N 3	Lee st E8	
6 N 12	Leeke st WC1	
12 T 8	Lees pl W1	
13 G 9	Leicester ct WC2	
13 G 9	Leicester pl WC2	
13 G 10	Leicester sq WC2	
13 F 9	Leicester st WC2	
1 C 9	Leigh gdns NW10	
15 A 17	Leigh Hunt st SE1	
14 T 1	Leigh pl EC1	
5 J 15	Leigh st WC1	
1 C 7	Leighton gdns NW10	
11 B 7	Leinster gdns W2	
11 B 10	Leinster ms W2	
11 A 7	Leinster pl W2	
2 T 12	Leinster rd NW6	
10 W 7	Leinster sq W2	
11 B 10	Leinster ter W2	
2 U 4	Leith yd NW6	
8 S 5	Lelitia clo E8	
16 R 17	Leman st E1	
17 D 2	Lena gdns W6	
20 N 4	Lennox Gdns ms SW1	
20 N 4	Lennox gdns SW1	
19 B 5	Lenthall pl SW7	
24 U 10	Lenville way SE16	
24 Z 17	Leo st SE15	
6 Y 18	Leo yd EC1	
7 F 16	Leonard st EC2	
24 T 19	Leontine clo SE15	
22 N 10	Leopold wlk SE11	
23 J 3	Leroy st SE1	
18 N 19	Letterstone rd SW6	
7 A 14	Lever st EC1	
6 Y 14	Lever st EC1	
19 M 6	Leverett st SW3	
13 G 19	Lewisham st SW1	
18 Y 4	Lexham Gdns ms W8	
18 X 4	Lexham gdns W8	
18 V 4	Lexham ms W8	
18 Y 3	Lexham wlk W8	
13 D 8	Lexington st W1	
15 M 3	Leyden st E1	
16 N 3	Leyden st E1	
14 X 19	Library st SE1	
1 C 7	Liddell gdns NW10	
5 B 10	Lidlington pl NW1	
3 K 17	Lilestone st NW8	
18 V 13	Lillie Bridge ms SW6	
17 H 16	Lillie rd SW6	
18 P 14	Lillie rd SW6	
18 U 13	Lillie yd SW6	
21 D 8	Lillington Gdn est SW1	
17 J 8	Lily clo W14	
10 V 11	Lime ct W8	
9 B 16	Lime gro W12	
15 J 7	Lime st EC3	
19 D 14	Limestone st SW10	
24 T 18	Limpston Gdn est SE15	
2 N 3	Lincoln ms NW6	
20 O 8	Lincoln st SW3	
14 O 5	Lincolns Inn fields WC2	
1 E 11	Linden av NW10	
10 V 11	Linden gdns W2	
10 U 11	Linden ms W2	
16 Z 1	Lindley st E1	
14 Y 1	Lindsey st EC1	
4 N 18	Linhope st NW1	
24 S 5	Linsey st SE16	
7 C 5	Linton st N1	
1 K 20	Lionel ms W10	
18 N 6	Lisgar ter W14	
13 G 9	Lisle st WC2	
3 G 15	Lisson gro NW8	
3 K 20	Lisson st NW1	
22 X 20	Listowell clo SW9	
22 X 20	Listowell st SW9	
13 H 8	Litchfield st WC2	
24 Y 5	Litlington st SE16	
4 Z 14	Little Albany st NW1	
13 A 6	Little Argyll st W1	
18 Z 10	Little Boltons the SW5	
19 A 11	Little Boltons the SW10	
15 A 3	Little Britain EC1	
14 Y 2	Little Britain EC1	
12 W 20	Little Chester st SW1	
21 J 2	Little College st SW1	
15 C 16	Little Dorrit ct SE1	
14 R 8	Little Essex st WC2	
14 R 8	Little Essex st WC2	
13 J 19	Little George st SW1	
13 B 7	Little Marlborough st W1	
14 V 5	Little New st EC4	
13 G 9	Little Newport st WC2	
13 A 4	Little Portland st W1	
13 J 2	Little Russell st WC1	
13 H 19	Little Sanctuary SW1	
21 H 2	Little Smith st SW1	
16 N 6	Little Somerset st E1	
13 B 15	Little St. James st SW1	
13 A 3	Little Titchfield st W1	
14 N 3	Little Turnstile WC1	
23 C 11	Liverpool gro SE17	
6 U 2	Liverpool rd N1	
15 K 2	Liverpool St station EC2	
15 J 2	Liverpool st EC2	
24 T 14	Livesey pl SE15	
13 D 7	Livonia st W1	
7 C 15	Lizard st EC1	
16 T 18	Llewellyn st SE16	
6 S 12	Lloyd Baker st WC1	
6 R 13	Lloyd sq WC1	
6 S 12	Lloyd st WC1	
15 K 7	Lloyds av EC3	
6 V 13	Lloyds row EC1	
17 E 13	Lochaline st W6	
24 W 2	Lockwood sq SE16	
15 F 18	Lockyer st SE1	
3 H 15	Lodge rd NW8	
16 U 18	Loftie st SE16	
6 S 1	Lofting rd N1	
18 T 5	Logan ms W8	
18 T 5	Logan pl W8	
22 S 7	Lollard st SE11	
14 Y 16	Loman st SE11	
8 U 19	Lomas st S1	
14 U 7	Lombard la EC4	
15 G 7	Lombard st EC3	
10 Y 10	Lombardy pl W2	
23 D 19	Lomond gro SE5	
23 L 13	Loncroft st SE5	
15 F 12	London br EC4	
15 F 14	London Br st SE1	
15 H 14	London Bridge station SE1	
8 W 2	London Fields East side E8	
11 G 5	London ms W2	
22 X 2	London rd SE1	
15 K 8	London st EC3	
11 G 6	London st W2	
15 G 3	London wall EC2	
13 L 6	Long acre WC2	
14 Y 1	Long la EC1	
15 D 18	Long la SE1	
7 M 11	Long st E2	
23 L 1	Long wlk SE1	
6 N 18	Long yd WC1	
4 Z 16	Longford st NW1	
24 S 10	Longland ct SE1	
24 S 6	Longley st SE1	
21 B 7	Longmore st SW1	
18 T 7	Longridge rd SW5	
13 G 11	Longs ct WC2	
22 X 5	Longville rd SE11	
6 U 2	Lonsdale pl N1	
2 O 6	Lonsdale rd NW6	
10 R 7	Lonsdale rd W11	
6 T 2	Lonsdale sq N1	
2 Y 20	Lord Hills rd W2	
21 J 2	Lord North st SW1	
18 X 19	Lord Roberts ms SW6	
8 P 13	Lorden wlk E2	
3 G 13	Lords Cricket grd NW8	
19 K 15	Lordship pl SW3	
6 O 11	Lorenzo st WC1	

O

12 W 16	Old Park la W1	
21 F 1	Old Pye st SW1	
12 R 7	Old Quebec st W1	
13 G 19	Old Queen st SW1	
14 W 5	Old Seacoal la EC4	
21 L 18	Old South Lambeth rd SW8	
14 R 4	Old sq WC2	
7 J 14	Old st EC1	
4 T 19	Oldbury pl W1	
1 K 11	Oliphant st W10	
7 F 17	Olivers yd EC2	
24 R 13	Olmar st SE1	
23 A 14	Olney rd SE17	
22 Z 14	Olney st SE17	
17 M 3	Olympia rd W14	
17 L 4	Olympia W14	
10 Z 9	Olympia yd W2	
5 M 10	Omega pl N1	
18 T 13	Ongar rd SW6	
19 E 8	Onslow gdns SW7	
19 F 7	Onslow Ms east SW7	
19 E 8	Onslow Ms west SW7	
19 G 6	Onslow sq SW7	
6 U 19	Onslow st EC1	
22 Y 2	Ontario st SE1	
22 V 9	Opal st SE11	
4 O 2	Oppidans rd NW3	
4 O 1	Oppidans rd NW3	
13 F 11	Orange st WC2	
13 G 6	Orange yd W1	
23 E 8	Orb st SE17	
17 M 19	Orbain rd SW6	
12 T 8	Orchard st W1	
3 F 18	Orchardson st NW8	
6 N 19	Orde Hall st WC1	
3 G 6	Ordnance hill NW8	
3 H 8	Ordnance ms NW8	
22 W 4	Orient st SE11	
10 Y 10	Orme Ct ms W2	
10 Y 9	Orme ct W2	
10 X 10	Orme la W2	
10 X 10	Orme sq W2	
5 M 18	Ormond ms WC1	
13 C 12	Ormond yd SW1	
20 O 11	Ormonde ga SW1	
4 O 6	Ormonde ter NW8	
8 N 8	Ormsby st E2	
10 Z 4	Orsett ms W2	
10 Z 4	Orsett ms W2	
11 A 4	Orsett ms W2	
22 P 9	Orsett st SE11	
10 Z 4	Orsett ter W2	
11 A 4	Orsett ter W2	
7 L 5	Orsman rd N1	
16 T 14	Orton st E1	
21 E 7	Osbert st SW1	
8 S 5	Osborn cl E8	
16 P 3	Osborn st E1	
4 Z 16	Osnaburgh st NW1	
4 Z 17	Osnaburgh ter NW1	
12 T 1	Ossington bldgs W1	
10 W 11	Ossington st W2	
24 R 12	Ossory rd SE1	
5 F 11	Ossulston st NW1	
18 Z 3	Osten ms SW7	
22 X 4	Oswin st SE11	
22 W 9	Othello clo SE11	
22 W 14	Otto st SE17	
3 M 11	Outer circle NW1 & NW8	
4 W 10	Outer circle NW1 & NW8	
5 L 4	Outram st N1	
15 K 4	Outwhich st EC3	
22 R 14	Oval Cricket grd SE11	
4 X 5	Oval rd NW1	
8 W 8	Oval the E2	
22 P 12	Oval way SE11	
17 B 5	Overstone rd W6	
19 L 2	Ovington gdns SW3	
19 M 2	Ovington ms SW3	

19 M 2	Ovington sq SW3	
19 M 4	Ovington st SW3	
20 N 5	Ovington st SW3	
6 V 11	Owen st EC1	
6 W 11	Owens ct EC1	
6 V 11	Owens row EC1	
13 F 10	Oxendon st SW1	
13 A 6	Oxford Cir av W1	
13 A 6	Oxford cir W1	
9 J 4	Oxford gdns W10	
2 W 7	Oxford rd NW6	
11 L 6	Oxford sq W1	
13 E 4	Oxford st W1	
12 T 17	Oxford st W1	

P

16 Y 7	Pace pl E1	
7 A 6	Packington sq N1	
6 Y 4	Packington st N1	
8 P 14	Padbury ct E2	
11 G 1	Paddington grn W2	
12 S 1	Paddington st W1	
11 F 6	Paddington station W2	
21 G 5	Page st SW1	
23 L 3	Pages wlk SE1	
6 W 12	Paget st EC1	
6 P 15	Pakenham st WC1	
10 Z 7	Palace av W8	
10 W 10	Palace ct W2	
11 B 19	Palace ga W8	
10 W 12	Palace Gdns ms W8	
10 W 14	Palace Gdns ter W8	
10 Y 17	Palace gen W8	
20 U 7	Palace ms SW1	
21 B 2	Palace st SW1	
22 R 17	Palfrey pl SW8	
8 O 14	Palissy st E2	
13 G 13	Pall Mall east SW1	
13 C 14	Pall Mall pl SW1	
13 E 14	Pall Mall SW1	
17 K 10	Palliser rd W14	
3 G 16	Pallitt dri NW8	
13 D 20	Palmer st SW1	
21 E 1	Palmer st SW1	
9 F 6	Pamber st W10	
5 E 7	Pancras rd NW1	
9 D 1	Pangbourne av W10	
13 G 10	Panton st WC2	
14 T 8	Paper bldng EC4	
20 S 16	Parade the SW11	
16 Y 19	Paradise st SE16	
20 P 13	Paradise wlk SW3	
6 Y 16	Pardon st EC1	
15 G 20	Pardoner st SE1	
16 U 4	Parfett st E1	
17 E 13	Parfrey st W6	
14 V 13	Paris gdn SE1	
4 W 19	Park Cres Ms east W1	
4 Y 18	Park Cres Ms east W1	
4 X 18	Park cres W1	
13 B 14	Park pl SW1	
3 D 20	Park Pl vlls W2	
4 O 17	Park rd NW1	
3 L 13	Park rd NW8	
4 X 17	Park Sq east NW1	
4 W 17	Park Sq ms NW1	
4 W 17	Park Sq west NW1	
15 B 12	Park st SE1	
12 S 7	Park st W1	
12 T 11	Park st W1	
4 Y 9	Park Village east NW1	
4 X 8	Park Village west NW1	
11 L 5	Park West pl W2	
19 D 13	Park wlk SW10	
13 M 4	Parker st WC2	

16 R 19	Parkers row SE1	
6 U 8	Parkfield st N1	
19 K 20	Parkgate rd SW11	
23 G 17	Parkhouse st SE5	
18 O 19	Parkville rd SW6	
4 X 5	Parkway NW1	
13 J 19	Parliament sq SW1	
13 J 18	Parliament st SW1	
8 Y 8	Parmiter pl E2	
8 Y 9	Parmiter st E2	
7 D 7	Parr st N1	
21 K 14	Parry st SW8	
21 H 18	Pascal st SW8	
20 T 8	Passmore st SW1	
22 Y 4	Pastor st SE11	
18 T 2	Pater st W8	
14 Y 5	Paternoster sq EC4	
22 W 20	Patmos rd SW9	
7 A 14	Paton st EC1	
8 Y 10	Patriot sq E2	
7 H 18	Paul st EC2	
19 H 14	Paultons sq SW3	
19 H 15	Paultons st SW3	
19 J 19	Paveley dr SW11	
3 L 15	Paveley st NW8	
12 P 20	Pavilion rd SW1	
20 P 4	Pavilion rd SW1	
20 P 3	Pavilion st SW1	
17 K 14	Paynes wk W6	
20 X 10	Peabody av SW1	
20 Y 12	Peabody clo SW1	
21 F 11	Peabody estate SW1	
8 T 17	Peace st E1	
22 Y 8	Peacock st SE17	
22 Z 8	Peacock yd SE17	
14 T 17	Pear pl SE1	
6 U 17	Pear Tree ct EC1	
4 A 15	Pear Tree st EC1	
6 Z 15	Pear Tree st EC1	
14 T 19	Pearman st SE1	
8 N 8	Pearson st E2	
7 M 8	Pearson st E2	
23 K 18	Peckham gro SE15	
24 R 19	Peckham Hill st SE15	
24 U 14	Peckham Pk rd SE15	
8 S 10	Peel Precinct ct NW6	
10 U 14	Peel st W8	
7 E 14	Peerless st EC1	
22 S 13	Pegasus pl SE11	
19 J 7	Pelham cres SW7	
19 J 6	Pelham pl SW7	
19 J 6	Pelham st SW7	
23 B 13	Pelier st SE17	
17 M 16	Pellant rd SW6	
8 N 12	Pelter st E2	
1 F 13	Pember rd NW10	
14 U 5	Pemberton row EC4	
10 S 9	Pembridge cres W11	
10 U 11	Pembridge gdns W2	
10 S 9	Pembridge ms W11	
10 U 8	Pembridge pl W2	
10 T 10	Pembridge rd W11	
10 U 9	Pembridge sq W2	
10 T 8	Pembridge vlls W11	
12 U 18	Pembroke clo SW1	
18 S 4	Pembroke Gdns clo W8	
18 S 5	Pembroke gdns W8	
18 T 3	Pembroke ms W8	
18 T 2	Pembroke pl W8	
18 R 6	Pembroke rd W14	
18 T 4	Pembroke sq W8	
5 M 3	Pembroke st N1	
18 R 3	Pembroke studios W8	
18 T 4	Pembroke vlls W8	
18 T 4	Pembroke wlk W8	
7 F 4	Penally pl N1	
16 Y 12	Penang st E1	
24 V 15	Pencraig way SE15	
3 J 20	Penfold pl NW1	

18 R 11	Stanier clo W14
9 A 14	Stanlake rd W12
9 A 15	Stanlake vlls W12
22 N 16	Stanley clo SW8
10 O 9	Stanley cres W11
10 P 9	Stanley gdns W11
5 J 9	Stanley pas NW1
6 N 3	Stanmore st N1
22 U 12	Stannary pl SE11
22 U 13	Stannary st SE11
23 K 20	Stanswood gdns SE5
7 K 9	Stanway st N1
18 O 7	Stanwick rd W14
14 S 3	Staple Inn bldgs WC1
14 S 3	Staple Inn WC1
15 G 19	Staple st SE1
15 K 8	Star all EC3
18 O 12	Star rd W14
11 J 4	Star st W2
14 S 5	Star yd WC2
5 C 14	Starcross st NW1
24 X 11	Starkleigh way SE16
24 X 10	Starkleigh way SE16
1 E 9	Station ter NW10
14 Y 6	Stationers Hall ct EC4
23 D 7	Stead st SE17
8 N 4	Stean st E8
13 J 3	Stedham pl WC1
22 Z 7	Steedman st SE17
8 U 4	Stephan clo E8
13 E 3	Stephen ms W1
13 E 3	Stephen st W1
5 C 15	Stephensons way NW1
16 W 2	Stepney way E1
11 L 20	Sterling st SW7
17 E 2	Sterndale rd W14
9 F 16	Sterne st W12
15 E 19	Sterry st SE1
17 E 20	Stevenage rd SW6
7 M 20	Steward st E1
15 L 1	Steward st E1
19 J 9	Stewarts gro SW3
20 Z 20	Stewarts la SW8
21 A 20	Stewarts st SW8
21 C 4	Stillington st SW2
14 R 3	Stone bldgs WC2
15 K 3	Stone House ct E3
14 V 4	Stonecutter st EC4
6 T 4	Stonefield st N1
9 H 10	Stoneleigh pl W11
9 H 10	Stoneleigh st W11
15 A 19	Stones End st SE1
15 M 4	Stoney la E1
15 D 13	Stoney st SE1
15 P 7	Stonor rd W14
22 Z 11	Stopford rd SE17
13 H 19	Store st WC1
13 H 19	Storeys ga SW1
24 U 3	Storks rd SE16
6 N 3	Story st N1
12 N 5	Stourcliffe st W1
13 L 10	Strand WC2
14 P 8	Strand WC2
18 O 2	Strangways rd W14
5 M 3	Stranraer way N1
12 V 6	Stratford pl W1
18 V 4	Stratford rd W8
18 V 3	Stratford studios W8
11 J 8	Strathearn pl W2
10 V 13	Strathmore gdns W8
24 T 7	Strathnairn st SE1
12 Z 13	Stratton st W1
13 H 3	Streatham st WC1
2 P 1	Streatley rd NW6
17 K 17	Strode rd SW6
8 N 12	Stronts pl E2
21 E 3	Strutton ground SW1

15 M 2	Strype st E1
2 U 14	Stuart rd NW6
4 Y 1	Stucley st NW1
6 W 4	Studd st N1
24 X 18	Studholme sr SE15
12 R 18	Studio pl SW1
13 L 4	Stukeley st WC2
14 Z 17	Sturge st SE1
22 Z 11	Sturgeon rd SE17
7 B 19	Sturt st N1
16 U 7	Stutfield st E1
6 X 9	Sudeley st N1
15 A 18	Sudrey st SE1
13 F 12	Suffolk pl SW1
13 F 12	Suffolk st SW1
23 E 16	Sugden st SE5
9 D 19	Sulgrave rd W6
17 C 1	Sulgrave rd W6
22 V 5	Sullivan rd SE11
23 A 18	Sultan st SE5
1 M 8	Summerfield av NW6
2 N 8	Summerfield av NW6
6 T 18	Summers st EC1
19 G 6	Sumner Pl ms SW7
19 G 7	Sumner pl SW7
24 O 15	Sumner rd SE15
14 Z 13	Sumner st SE1
15 A 13	Sumner st SE1
18 O 12	Sun rd W14
7 H 20	Sun st EC2
7 J 20	Sun St pas EC2
15 J 1	Sun St pas EC2
10 W 5	Sunderland ter W2
2 V 18	Surrendale pl W9
14 X 17	Surrey row SE1
23 K 8	Surrey sq SE17
14 P 8	Surrey st WC2
11 H 6	Sussex gdns W2
11 H 8	Sussex Ms east W2
11 G 9	Sussex Ms west W2
4 O 16	Sussex pl NW1
11 H 7	Sussex pl W2
17 C 9	Sussex pl W6
11 G 8	Sussex sq W2
20 Z 10	Sussex st SW1
2 V 19	Sutherland av W9
3 B 15	Sutherland av W9
10 T 5	Sutherland pl W2
20 Y 9	Sutherland row SW1
23 A 12	Sutherland sq SE17
20 Z 11	Sutherland st SW1
23 B 12	Sutherland wlk SE17
13 F 5	Sutton row W1
1 B 19	Sutton way W10
12 Z 6	Swallow pas W1
13 C 11	Swallow st W1
23 J 3	Swan mead SE1
15 C 19	Swan st SE1
15 F 11	Swan wharf EC4
20 O 14	Swan wlk SW3
8 O 15	Swanfield st E2
9 H 14	Swanscombe rd W11
16 V 9	Swedenborg gdns E1
16 O 19	Sweeney cres SE1
10 N 1	Swinbrook rd W10
9 A 14	Swindon st W12
6 N 13	Swinton pl WC1
6 O 12	Swinton st WC1
9 A 20	Sycamore gdns W6
7 A 17	Sycamore st EC1
19 H 8	Sydney clo SW3
19 H 7	Sydney ms SW3
19 H 7	Sydney pl SW7
19 J 8	Sydney st SW3
24 Y 16	Sylvan gro SE15
20 P 6	Symons st SW3

T

15 D 18	Tabard st SE1
23 F 1	Tabard st SE1

7 G 18	Tabernacle st EC2
21 B 6	Tachbrook ms SW1
21 E 9	Tachbrook st SW1
19 C 18	Tadema rd SW10
9 E 15	Tadmor st W12
10 P 6	Talbot rd W11
10 U 4	Talbot rd W2
11 G 6	Talbot sq W2
15 F 15	Talbot yd SE1
17 J 9	Talgarth rd W14
14 U 8	Tallis st EC4
2 S 16	Tamplin ms W9
18 T 14	Tamworth st SW6
5 L 13	Tankerton st WC1
16 O 18	Tanner st SE1
15 K 18	Tanner st SE1
14 T 18	Tanswell st SE1
7 B 10	Taplow st N1
8 X 17	Tapp st E1
16 Y 6	Tarling st E1
22 Y 10	Tarver rd SE17
17 K 14	Tasso rd W6
21 J 7	Tate gallery SW1
23 G 7	Tatum st SE17
4 O 18	Taunton ms NW1
4 N 17	Taunton pl NW1
9 K 15	Taverners clo W11
10 O 2	Tavistock cres W10
10 N 5	Tavistock ms W11
5 H 16	Tavistock pl WC1
10 O 3	Tavistock rd W11
5 G 16	Tavistock sq WC1
14 N 7	Tavistock st WC2
13 M 9	Tavistock st WC2
5 F 16	Taviton st WC1
5 M 2	Tayport clo N1
8 U 8	Teale st E2
20 N 11	Tedworth gdns SW3
20 N 11	Tedworth sq SW3
8 V 10	Teesdale yd E2
18 R 14	Telephone pl W14
1 K 20	Telford rd W10
14 U 8	Temple av EC4
14 U 7	Temple la EC4
14 P 9	Temple pl WC2
8 V 9	Temple st E2
8 Z 3	Templecombe rd E9
18 U 6	Templeton pl SW5
16 W 13	Tench st E1
24 V 8	Tenda rd SE16
13 B 8	Tenison ct W1
14 R 14	Tenison way SE1
11 A 8	Tenniel clo W2
15 E 17	Tennis st SE1
2 P 5	Tennyson rd SW6
8 V 17	Tent st E1
16 N 2	Tenter ground E1
12 Y 6	Tenterden st W1
20 Z 4	Terminus pl SW1
2 S 3	Terrace the NW6
20 P 16	Terrace wlk SW11
6 W 2	Terretts pl N1
6 V 6	Tetbury pl N1
24 U 10	Tetterby way SE16
10 Y 20	Thackeray st W8
5 J 14	Thanet st WC1
14 U 3	Thavies in EC4
18 R 13	Thaxton rd SW6
12 U 4	Thayer st W1
6 V 4	Theberton st N1
14 T 14	Theed st SE1
23 E 3	Theobald st SE1
6 O 20	Theobalds rd WC1
21 A 19	Thessally rd SW8
1 M 15	Third av W10
21 C 3	Thirleby rd SW1
19 C 9	Thistle gro SW5
22 X 1	Thomas Doyle st SE1
16 S 12	Thomas More st SE1
24 S 7	Thorburn sq SE1
7 B 11	Thoresby st N1
21 J 19	Thorncroft st SW8

Y

Z